INFORMATION SYSTEMS

□

Management Practices in Action

ROBERT K. WYSOCKI

JAMES YOUNG

INFORMATION SYSTEMS

Management Practices
in Action

Wiley Series in Computing and Information Processing

Hugh J. Watson, University of Georgia-Athens, Series Editor

INFORMATION SYSTEMS

Management Practices in Action

*A Collection
of Management Situations*

ROBERT K. WYSOCKI

Bentley College

JAMES YOUNG

Wheeler Group

JOHN WILEY & SONS

New York □ Chichester □ Brisbane □ Toronto □ Singapore

Drawings Rich Tennant

Library of Congress Cataloging in Publication Data:

Wysocki, Robert K.
    Information systems : management practices in action : a collection of
management situations / Robert K. Wysocki, James Young.

          p.   cm.
    Bibliography: p.
    ISBN 0-471-50374-6
    1. Management information systems—Case studies.   I. Young, James,
    1947-   . II. Title.

    T58.6.W97   1990
    658.4'038—dc20

Printed in the United States of America

10 9 8 7 6 5 4 3 2 1

about the authors

□

ROBERT K. WYSOCKI, PH.D.

Dr. Wysocki is the Director of the MBA Program and Adjunct Associate Professor of Computer Information Systems at Bentley College. He has more than 20 years of professional experience as an educator and administrator in graduate business programs, as an independent consultant, and as an internal systems consultant for Texas Instruments, Inc. He has several years of experience as an information systems manager and had developed and implemented two degree programs in computer and information systems. An active member of the Data Processing Management Association, he has several journal publications and professional presentations in the areas of information systems and management sciences. He holds degrees in mathematics and mathematical statistics from the University of Dallas and Southern Methodist University, respectively.

JAMES YOUNG

Mr. Young is the Vice President of Information and Telecommunications Systems for the Wheeler Group, a unit of Pitney Bowes in Hartford, Connecticut. His 17 years of experience includes data processing management positions in government (U.S. Marine Corps), management consulting (Arthur Young), and private industry (Barry Wright) as well as other management assignments. He has worked in a diversity of environments; large mainframe, minicomputer, and microcomputer, both centralized and decentralized.

Mr. Young holds degrees in engineering (B.S. from the U.S. Naval Academy), computer science (M.S. from the U.S. Naval Postgraduate School), business administration (M.B.A. from the Havard Business School) and the CDP. He frequently speaks on professional issues to groups such as ASM, EDPAA, IBM, Netron, and others. Mr. Young has written extensively on data processing issues and has been a contributing columnist for Computerworld since 1983. He is also currently visiting lecturer on MIS concepts in the graduate program of Clark University in Worcester, Massachusetts.

preface

☐

Having written a textbook on the management of information systems, we felt that the job was only half done. In the pages of the textbook we expound on the concepts, principles, and challenges facing the information systems manager. Knowing these is certainly prerequisite to being an effective information systems manager, but the lesson would not be complete without challenging the student with the application. Such is the purpose of this companion text.

In the pages of this book we have tried to capture the experiences we and our colleagues have had in discharging our duties as information systems managers. It is important that we share these experiences, for the student must understand that concepts and principles can be made to fit comfortably between the pages of the textbook but are quite a different matter when cast into real-world situations. For the information systems manager, the resolution of management problems at the corporate, functional, and end-user levels is exceedingly complex. Oftentimes there are several alternatives to choose from, with each one seeming to be wrong for one reason or another. It is here that "the rubber meets the road" and the information systems manager meets his or her true test.

These situations are designed to be used in conjunction with the text, *Information Systems: Management Principles In Action.* They are realistic examples of information systems management in practice. In most cases they have been generalized so as to provide a richer discussion opportunity and as an accompaniment to class lectures. In many cases there is no correct answer and the discussion will center around evaluating alternative decisions the information systems manager might make and the consequences of those decisions. An Instructor's Manual is written to accompany this book so that the instructor might see the richness of each Situation. We have chosen this way to document our use of these Situations for our students so that you might benefit from our experiences. We hope you enjoy the funny names and the lively discussion that will follow.

contents

□ .

ix

PART II

INFORMATION SYSTEMS
AS A CORPORATE ENTITY   13

chapter three

The role of information sysytems
as a corporate entity   15

chapter four

Information technology
as a competitive weapon   23

PART I

OVERVIEW OF INFORMATION SYSTEMS MANAGEMENT

one
□

Scope and Role of Information Systems Management

SITUATION 1-1

CHRIS P. SPUD POTATO CHIP COMPANY

You are Ida Hough, president and sole owner of the Chris P. Spud Potato Chip Company, a highly successful regional maker and distributor of snack-food products. Last year revenue grew to more than $15 million and, with your plans for new products and new marketing and distribution techniques, business promises to keep growing. Consequentially, you are anxious to ensure that all your departments are prepared to keep up with this growth.

The one function you are unsure of is the data-processing area. Right now, you do not have one. All financial reports are prepared by a service bureau based on batch input employees send them. This includes all invoices, vendor checks, and payroll checks. Turn-around on these is overnight and seems satisfactory. Queries into company data are done interactively through terminals leased from the service bureau so employees can check vendor and customer account information. Little else is automated. You do not object to automation, but your managers rarely ask for technical improvements to their current manual operations.

Your current data-processing service bureau costs about $20,000 a month, depending on how much is done for the company. On the knowledgeable advice of your public accounting firm, you are convinced that establishing an in-house data-processing function would cost about the same, so now is not the time to do it to save money. The service bureau is a very reliable firm and has discussed its willingness to provide expanded service, new applications, higher volumes, and so forth. However, as you sit there looking at your bill and considering what you are receiving today, you wonder if there are other factors to weigh before making a decision.

1. What are some of the advantages of bringing an IS function in house? What is the single most important factor?

2. What are some of the risks? Which one do you consider the biggest?

3. Should you wait until later when the change might be cost justified? How appropriate is using the least-cost alternative?

4. What course of action would you take?

SITUATION 1-2
WALLOP'S BREWING COMPANY

You are Darryl Licht, the president and CEO of the Wallop's Brewing Company, a small brewer of specialized, high quality beers and ales. ("Every bottle packs a Wallop" is your slogan.) You have just returned from the retirement party of Elka Hall, your IS manager for the last 25 years. Elka unexpectedly took early retirement in order to travel with her husband. In your congratulatory speech you correctly pointed out that she was instrumental in bringing computers to Wallop's, ensuring that they were thoroughly used, providing reliable service, and keeping costs under control. What you did not feel it appropriate to point out was that as a technician out of the old school, Elka ignored the latest technology in favor of the old "efficient ways" (only COBOL code could be used, for instance). She opposed personal computers and end-user computing and was very poor at recognizing and meeting strategic needs with your other executives. Elka was a dedicated, capable manager, but in your opinion did not change with the times.

Now you are faced with the problem of replacing Elka. You have narrowed the choice down to two internal candidates. Your preference, Marco DeStinkshun, would be a decided surprise to everyone because it is not a traditional appointment. He is now the Vice President of Strategic Planning but has had varied experience, all within Wallop's. Starting as a company salesman, he was promoted to customer service and then to product-line management. Before his current assignment Marco was Advertising Manager, earning his current job by virtue of his fresh, effective ideas, good working relations with people, and his ability to get things done. As Vice President of Strategic Planning, Marco had many ideas for innovative uses of information technology, most of which Elka had thrown cold water on. Marco was a personal computer enthusiast who used them heavily and advocated them for others as well. Marco may be a little impetuous and exuberant, but you like his ideas and think he is a good people-oriented manager. He will not be intimidated by the assignment. On the other hand, he has never managed technology before or even a department as large as IS. Moreover, he is seen as kind of a crackpot by the current IS staff.

Throughout the company, everyone expects that the job will go to Elka's right-hand man, Chip O'Silicon. Chip is currently Manager of Systems and Programming and is reputed to be a technical wizard. He has not been too happy that Elka has not kept Wallop's up-to-date technically and wants to do a lot more things. He is happiest when there are a lot of projects going on. However, Chip is a traditionalist; mainframe computing, programmer written systems, central control, and so on, and as such was eager to follow Elka's direction in the use of heavy-handed controls. Chip is highly respected within IS. You feel that were Chip to be the IS manager it would be Elka all over again, though he would be more responsive to your direction and not as stubborn as Elka. Moreover, Chip has experience in several other companies (unlike Marco) before coming to Wallop's 7 years ago.

There is little doubt in your mind that you would like to appoint Marco as the IS manager, relieving him of strategic-planning duties. You would like to get more high-level returns from IS. However, before you make up your mind, you want to make sure that this move will not cause operational damage. Wallop's depends heavily on existing IS systems that Elka kept running like a watch. That must continue or today's business will suffer.

1. What are some of the strengths Marco would bring to the job? What are the dangers of appointing Marco as IS manager?

2. Conversely, what are the strengths Chip could bring to the job? What areas of weakness raise the most concerns for you?

3. Is there a compromise solution that would gain the advantages while avoiding many of the problems?

4. Do both candidates have serious enough weaknesses to require you to look for an external candidate? What would the disadvantages of this approach be?

5. What would your decision be?

6. How would you go about effecting the change?

7. Are you too late in considering this choice? What might you have done if this decision were considered a year before Elka's retirement?

two

□

Foundation of
Information Systems
Management

SITUATION 2-1
BADEN-BADEN WAGEN MACHEN

Otto Makur is the President of Baden-Baden Wagen Machen (BWM), a well-respected German automobile manufacturer. The company is small compared to its competition but has built a solid reputation on the fact that its cars are hand-crafted even though they use rather dated technology. Otto has strongly resisted using computer technology reasoning "Mein Grossvater hat diese Firma mit traditionellen Methoden sum Erfolg gefuhrt. Ich habe nicht die Absicht diese Erfolgs-Strategie zu andern." (Loosely translated: It ain't broke, don't fix it.)

You are, Moe Turoil, the Vice President of Information Services at Goliath Car Manufacturer (GCM), the largest automobile manufacturer in the United States. GCM has just bought BWM. Otto was close to retirement and, to his disappointment, the family was not interested in continuing with the business. As part of the purchase,

GCM executives have agreed to let Otto and his employees continue on until Otto's retirement (in about 5 years), at which time GCM may elect to restructure BWM. You have just been instructed by Sue Barrue, the President of GCM and your boss, to develop and implement an information systems plan for bringing BWM into conformance with GCM. Whatever plan you choose to implement, it must preserve the hand-crafted manufacturing process at BWM. GCM expects to build a major marketing program that emphasizes quality and workmanship as an attempt to regain their former credibility and soundness as a quality company. BWM will become their showpiece for that new marketing program.

You have not spoken to the management team at BWM but have been able to learn a few facts about their operation and their use of computers. BWM employees are very loyal, and the turnover is low. The key operations level managers are long-time employees, all have more than 25-years experience at BWM. None of them, nor any of the senior managers, use computers. At the present time the accounting department uses a small minicomputer to do ledger, receivables, payables, and payroll. They purchased the system along with the software package about 5 years ago. There have been a few modifications to the software, which is all contracted out to the vendor. Service has been reliable, and the system meets the needs of the accounting department. You have found no other use, or even a request for use, of computers.

1. Was it wise for Sue Barrue to direct the development of an IS plan to bring BWM into conformance with GCM?

2. What issues will you have to consider in developing an IS plan for BWM?

3. What is your strategy for the first trip to BWM to meet their senior management team and discuss IS planning?

4. Why do you suspect there has been no request for use of computers at BWM?

SITUATION 2-2
DIGGS & HURTZ DENTAL CLINICS

You are Phil McCavety, the PC Supervisor at Diggs & Hurtz Dental Clinics, a regional chain offering walk-in services. The President, Perry O'Dontist, has just returned from a 3-day golf outing with other

members of the Young President's Club. Immediately on his return-
ing from the airport, he rushed to your office and announced that he
had learned about DBMSs and 4GLs at a special seminar held in
conjunction with the golf outing. He wanted to move immediately to
acquire and install the necessary hardware and software and get
going. He further explained that the seminar also included a presentation on using information technology to establish competitive
advantage. "It opened my eyes," he said. "I'm convinced that our
problems are all the result of our failure to keep up with the
technology. We're going to have to make up a lot of lost time. I'll send
you a folder this afternoon. It has all the information you need. Get
the hardware and software order in and let's get going!"

On your return to your cubicle you take stock of the situation.
Despite all your efforts in the past to get the clinic moving ahead with
the computer, you were never able to convince Perry that there was
any benefit to be gained. But now he is ready to charge ahead faster
than you feel would make good business sense. The only computer
use in the company is in the accounting department. You currently
supervise two data-entry clerks: one in payables and one in receivables. General ledger and payroll are the only two applications, and
they run on purchased software. There is a smattering of micros
across the clinic, but they are almost exclusively dedicated to word
processing. None of the clinic's staff currently have computer
equipment of any kind on their desk nor have any asked for any. You
happen to be familiar with Nolan's Stages Model and clearly position
yourself in the Initiation Stage. Perry clearly wants to jump to the
Data Administration Stage. You are pleased that the door is open to
make such a move but are a bit apprehensive.

1. What are the issues?

2. What actions are appropriate for the clinic?

3. What do you tell the President?

4. Under what circumstances might it be appropriate for an organization to move directly from the Initiation to the Data Administration stage?

PART II

INFORMATION SYSTEMS AS A CORPORATE ENTITY

three

The Role of Information Systems as a Corporate Entity

SITUATION 3-1
PIZZA DELIVERED QUICKLY, INC.

TO: All Operating Personnel, PDQ, Inc.

FROM: P. D. Que, President

SUBJECT: SYSTEM STUDY

Recently our competition has begun using computers to process the ordering and delivery of their pizzas. As a result, our business has dropped off by about the same amount as theirs has increased. We need to start using computers to improve operations and subsequently regain lost business. We have commissioned a system study under the leadership of Pepe Ronee, our senior operations analyst.

This approach will be a continuing long-range program that could extend over several years. Members of Pepe's department will be calling on you to discuss your current operations. Your cooperation as well as your support is essential to our defining systems needs accurately.

Most of you are unfamiliar with the computer and may wish to learn some basic fundamentals. This will help all of us understand how we can use computers to advantage. Pepe will be scheduling a series of short courses on Friday afternoons. In addition, you are welcome to take, at company expense, courses offered at Ivory Tower University. Check with your supervisor if you are interested.

It is important for each of us to remember that a successful computerization of our pizza delivery business will require your assistance. Computer systems have become very sophisticated, but rest assured, they will never replace your initiative and creative energies. I know you will want to do everything you can to contribute to a successful transition to the computer.

(Signed)

P. D. Que

1. What does this memo indicate concerning P. D. Que's involvement in the computer project?

2. What should he have done differently?

3. What should Pepe Ronee do as follow-up to the memo? Take into account the likely reactions of PDQ's personnel to the memo.

SITUATION 3-2
FLEET-O-FOOT SHOE COMPANY

You are Sally Forth, the Vice President of IS at Fleet-O-Foot. The company manufactures a full line of athletic shoes that are distributed through a nationwide network of manufacturer representatives. Business has been falling off dramatically for the past six quarters. It is generally agreed that part of the problem is attributable to the aggressive pricing strategy of a number of Southeast

Asian companies that recently introduced their product line into the American markets.

Hy Topps, the President of Fleet-O-Foot, has called you and the other vice presidents to an emergency management team retreat to determine an appropriate counterstrategy. As you take your seat at the opening session, you can not help but notice the somber expressions on the faces of the other vice presidents. Especially noticeable are Ann T. Lope, the Vice President of Sales and Marketing, and Manuel Labor, the Vice President of Manufacturing. You have not been privy to any earlier discussions on the problem, but it is very evident that the situation is grave. The room is deadly silent as Hy arrives, takes his seat, and begins the meeting.

"Thank you for clearing your calendars so that we could get away for a few days. We have a lot to do so I'll come right to the point. Sales, as most of you know, have continued to drop and the production backlog is critically low. While I'd be the first to agree that the incursion of our Oriental friends has been a factor, I've come to the conclusion that we're simply not doing our job. Let me be more specific.

"Our inventory levels have increased dramatically above their levels of the previous six quarters. I've satisfied myself that our sales forecasts are too optimistic and no longer believable.

"Production has been straightout trying to meet orders to inventory against these forecasts for our standard line, and as a result the special orders have been back-ordered or mis-shipped in far to many situations. Specifically, our returned material requests have doubled over the last three quarters."

You noticed Ann and Manuel sink deeper in their chairs as Hy glared at them while he spoke. You were waiting for your turn.

Hy continued, "Our position is desperate, and I want to know what you people intend to do about it. I want us back on track and fast!"

As you wonder how you were able to dodge the bullets your thoughts drifted back to the time when Manuel could not find the time to consider your proposal for the MRP system. You also recall how Ann stopped updating the forecast model parameters despite your continual reminders. In your opinion these systems could make a dramatic difference. As you recall, these as well as other situations, it hit you that you have hardly ever made it to first base with your proposals to Ann and Manuel. It now looks like you get the last laugh. But is that the kind of reaction Hy would expect of one of his senior managers or would he expect you to step forward with your proposals? As you size up the situation you have two alternatives. You can be proactive and offer your proposals in response to Hy's question. You can be reactive by taking some of the blame and propose working with Ann and Manuel to find a solution.

1. What are the possible consequences of each alternative?

2. Is it time to be proactive or reactive? Why?

3. What specific actions might you take?

SITUATION 3-3
FERDY LYSER SEED & GRAIN COOPERATIVE

You are Al Falpha, the new IS manager at Ferdy Lyser Seed & Grain Cooperative. You discovered after a few weeks on the job that Ferdy, the President of the Coop, was not completely honest with you during the interview. He characterized the previous IS manager, Molly Cottle, as a quiet, unassuming manager. Although Molly was very reliable and seldom missed a deadline, she never took a leadership role or suggested new systems and applications. According to Ferdy, the IS staff were relieved that Molly was gone and looked forward to assuming a more directive role in computing under your leadership.

You have found the staff to be quite different from what Ferdy led you to believe. (Ferdy did not intentionally misrepresent the situation, he simply did not understand it.) Without exception, every existing system was developed at user request. Operating in this environment for the past several years, the staff has become quite passive. They would rather do nothing than suggest new applications or improvements to existing applications. To meet Ferdy's expectations, you know that you will have to completely change the staff's attitude and orientation.

1. What are some of the things you need to do to make the staff proactive and take a more active role in the company?

2. Prioritize them and discuss your rationale for the assigned priorities.

3. Is it possible that the staff is beyond change and you might have to change personnel to meet your responsibilities?

SITUATION 3-4
RING & RUN ALARM SYSTEMS

May Cain and Bill Abel are the Vice Presidents of Manufacturing and Marketing, respectively, at Ring & Run. Ever since May was hired into this predominantly male-run company Bill has had a great deal of trouble getting along with her. Both are extremely well-qualified for their positions and tend to be very aggressive and results-oriented.

You are Olive Branch, the Vice President of Information Systems at Ring & Run. In general you have been able to work at the senior management level despite the fact that it is dominated by men. Although they are certainly courteous and professional in their dealings with you, you have always sensed some organizational distance. So many of the company's business decisions are made by the senior management team either on the golf course or at the hotel bar after work. You have never been invited to join them, although you would feel perfectly comfortable if asked to. May is the only other female senior manager, and you and she have commiserated on several occasions.

Fortunately you have been able to carry out your responsibilities without the gender issue becoming an obstacle. Recent developments have changed that however. For the past few years you have been watching a few vendors who offer specially adapted MRP systems for your industry. One of them has just announced a new release of their package that exactly matches your needs. Ring & Run desperately needs to replace its archaic inventory management software and you know that the President will want you to go ahead with the project. Your problem is how to deal with Bill and May. The new MRP system is such that you need their full cooperation if the conversion is to succeed. You have several alternatives:

1. Forge ahead with the project, ignoring the friction between Bill and May. After all, its their problem—let them work it out.

2. Call them both to a meeting at which you will appeal to their sense of responsibility as senior managers and hope that they will agree to bury the hatchet at least until the MRP system is installed.

3. Ignore them and work directly with their staff.

4. Hire an outside consultant (the vendor has offered to do a turnkey installation along with their necessary training).

5. Take the initiative with one of them and risk alienating the other.

6. Try to work around the problem by not involving them jointly at any point in time.

1. Consider each alternative. Which do you think is best and under what conditions?

2. How might you get them to buy in?

3. Can you identify any other courses of action?

four

□

Information Technology as a Competitive Weapon

SITUATION 4-1

BITS-N-BITES COFFEE SHOPS, INC.

You are Sal E. Vate, the IS manager at Bits-n-Bites, a regional chain of 6 coffee shops. Del E. Catessan, the business manager, called you to his office to discuss the extensive personal computing activity of Mike Rowtoys, his purchasing manager. You know that Mike has been one of your most active users and always seems to be calling your attention to new products and new applications. In fact, Mike has often been a good source of information for you on matters related to microcomputers. You recall that Bill was initially very supportive of Mike's getting involved with computers. In fact, Mike was almost single-handedly responsible for computerizing the business office. He is enthusiastic and quite willing to lend a hand on a computer problem whenever asked. Bill is concerned that Mike has become so involved with the computer that he is neglecting his job responsibilities and getting involved in computing activities that have no intrinsic value to the company or to the business office. Bill asked you to step in, find out what Mike is doing, and straighten him out.

1. How do you handle this situation so as not to come between Mike and Bill and yet not appear to be withdrawing your support and encouragement of personal computing?

2. Is what Mike doing inappropriate? In what ways might it have value to the company?

SITUATION 4-2
CUSTU-MAIL COMPANY (A)

Bill U. Slowly lost his job as the IS manager for Custu-Mail as a result of his failure to keep his company up to date in its use of information technology in the production and distribution of its products. As a result, the IS department is significantly behind the times and the company has suffered a severe loss of market share as the competition has been able to establish strategic advantage. You are I.M. Kwicker and were hired to replace Bill. You have been given a clear mandate and the appropriate authority to recapture market share through the use of the newer technologies.

Custu-Mail is a direct mail order house that custom designs and distributes executive and business gifts, promotions, and prizes. Their products are custom-made and range from plastic letter openers molded into the shape of a famous Washington landmark to a small carved wooden statue of a clown for a famous hamburger franchise. Products are usually sent directly to recipients by Custu-Mail on instructions from the customer. The business process is unique because it is conducted by mail or phone and proceeds as follows:

1. A stylish catalog displaying samples of Custu-Mail's products, prices, and special services (gift packing, special message, etc.) is produced.
2. The catalog is mass mailed to current and prospective customers. For the prospect list, Custu-Mail purchases mailing lists through a single broker. If people like what they see in the catalog, they discuss their needs with a telephone sales

representative and often initiate an order at the same time. Sample material is sent back and forth in the process of fabrication and customer approval of each unique product.

3. Once a product design is approved by the customer, Custu-Mail assigns a customer reference number that uniquely identifies both the product and the customer. This assures the manufacture of precisely the same product in the future.

4. In the future all the customer does is call or mail the order in, identifying themselves and the product by giving their customer reference number, tell where the custom products are to be sent, and give any other special instructions. Custu-Mail makes the products to order as quickly as possible, sends them out by the fastest means, and bills the customer.

This is the current process. As Custu-Mail tries to regain its market position it must consider modifying and improving the process. As it is your responsibility to determine such future enhancements, you have been watching several areas of technology that you think might offer prospects for improvement. You know that you will have to pay attention to the right technical areas in order to apply any enhancements as soon as practical.

1. How would you determine the broad areas that might offer technical promise for Custu-Mail? Prioritize these areas and discuss your rationale. Which of these technologies do you think might offer the greatest improvements to Custu-Mail?

2. Is it important for you to focus your attention on selected areas now, or can you afford to keep up with all of technology until a potential application breakthrough occurs?

3. What action will you take to keep up with the identified areas?

SITUATION 4-3
CUSTU-MAIL COMPANY (B)

Shortly after arriving at Custu-Mail you developed and distributed your plan for identifying areas of information technology use to reestablish the company's competitive position. You decided to solicit ideas from each of the senior and middle-level managers. Your approach was rather simple and the same for each manager:

1. Define the process (value chain).
2. Identify areas of need and possible application of information technology.
3. Meet with the manager responsible for some part of the process (preferably over lunch) and discuss your ideas.
4. Agree on a few areas of opportunity for further investigation.

Once this process was completed you planned to issue a comprehensive report outlining projects to be undertaken and the priorities for development.

Little did you realize just how your plan would unfold. Apparently the situation under Bill U. Slowly was much more serious than anyone would have guessed. The response from the managers was overwhelming. Their earlier disregard for information technology was more a reaction to Bill's style than it was to any lack of interest on their part. They were now very anxious to move ahead under your leadership. There was certainly no shortage of ideas either. The sum total of what was requested by the managers far exceeded the resources available to you. Managers had obviously given their requests some thought. Many, in fact, were presented in a thorough report accompanied by a complete needs analyses. You suspect that several of these reports may have been prepared and proposed to Bill but died for lack of interest on his part.

The project was so successful that the President took notice and commented to you, "I.M., I'm impressed with the way you so quickly involved the management team and brought them back to life. I was beginning to wonder if I would ever see that spark of enthusiasm again. I'm absolutely overwhelmed by all of the ideas that I'm hearing them discuss. I hope you have a plan as to how you're going to continue now that you've got everyone's attention and support. I'm not sure I grasp the full significance of what you've done or its potential impact on our business, but I'm leaving it up to you to propose a project plan consistent with our resources. In the meanwhile, I think its very important not to lose the momentum you have created. I think it would be truly unfortunate for all of us if the management team lost their enthusiasm a second time."

The President's comments gave you reason to pause and reflect. The managers are turned on. They have requested more than you can deliver. The president has taken an interest in what you have done and will be watching to see how you follow through. To back off and not deliver would not only be disappointing to them but it would also raise doubts as to your ability as a manager.

1. What are the risks in meeting all requests?

2. What are the risks in postponing some requests?

3. If you decide that doing some of the projects is the best strategy, how will you proceed?

4. How will you decide which projects to do and how will you prioritize them?

five

Strategic Information Systems Planning

SITUATION 5-1
L. E. BABA ORIENTAL IMPORTS

Anne Teak is the CEO at L. E. Baba and wants her executives to get involved in strategic IS planning. The company has been growing very rapidly owing to Anne's having installed an aggressive buying program that involved most of the senior managers. The company is organized along a number of specialty areas, with each senior manager responsible for one area. Although they do not have extensive travel schedules, their staffs do. Anne feels that a more directed buying program based on market niches currently served by L. E. Baba and trends in the import markets will give the company a better cash-flow position and hence increase net income.

You are E. Gerbeever, the IS manager, and are new to the company. Senior management has not shown much interest in information technology in the past. They always seem to be too busy and are often prone to sending a delegate rather than coming themselves. Although their delegates seem to look forward to these meetings, there does not seem to be good communications back to the senior managers and the delegates often change from meeting to meeting, so there is no continuity there either.

You know the importance of getting the senior managers involved from the start, but you are not sure of the best approach. You have identified the following alternatives:

1. If you do it, they may not take it seriously.
2. Hire a consultant to do it for you.
3. Send them away for executive education at the risk that they will not be receptive to the idea.

1. Compare and contrast each strategy.

2. Which would you choose and why?

3. For the chosen strategy, outline the implementation plan you would follow.

4. Can you think of another alternative for getting them involved?

5. What kind of involvement should Anne have in the process? How would you do it?

SITUATION 5-2
PONCE DE LEON NURSING HOMES, INC.

PAT PROPOSED A RATHER UNUSUAL MARKETING PROGRAM THAT WOULD REQUIRE EXTENSIVE SYSTEMS DEVELOPMENT.

Pat Rownizor is the Vice President of Marketing for a chain of nursing homes that have been unable to turn a profit for the past few years. The Board of Directors identified a number of problem areas, most of which are related to the fact that the operation is very inefficiently run and its people are not spending their time productively. With the help of a team of consultants from one of the big eight accounting firms, the Board developed a strategic plan that calls for a rather aggressive information systems upgrade. You are Jerry Atrick, an expert in the field of computers in nursing homes, and were approached by the Board because of your accomplishments. They were very aggressive in their recruiting and hiring of you and have given you the freedom to act as you see fit.

You report to Anita Kaskett, the President, which under most circumstances would give you some leverage and organizational parity with senior management. Unfortunately, Anita is nearing retirement and spends much of her day practicing on the putting green she installed in a vacant office adjoining her office suite. Although she does participate in day-to-day business affairs, depending on her may be somewhat risky. In any event, the Board expects you to turn the operation around within the next 3 years.

The first day on the job, you were approached by Pat, who proposed a rather unusual marketing program that would require an extensive systems development effort in order to be implemented. You told him that you would get back to him next week after you had a chance to get familiar with the operation and review his idea against the Board's strategic plan. After reviewing Pat's plan and the Board's plan you have concluded that Pat's idea, although it has a good chance of working, is not consistent with the Board's intentions. Furthermore, after talking with some of the other managers you strongly suspect that Pat is trying to use you (remember you are the new kid on the block) to get one of his pet projects implemented.

You have sized up the situation as follows. You need to get a project that you can be successful with to win the confidence and support of senior management and this project is a very likely candidate. Despite Pat's aggressive approach with you, you know that having his support would help you gain acceptance among the other senior managers. Your problem is that Pat's proposed system is not consistent with the corporate plan and it would be easily seen as such.

On the other hand, the previous IS manager had never had an opportunity to gain exposure at the senior management level and you do. In the past, the senior management team has been tough when it comes to their receptivity of information technology. Even though you are acting under mandate of the Board, you know that senior management will be reluctant to go along with your ideas and will instead look for other ways to meet the Board's strategic objectives.

1. Is there any reason to establish a relationship with the president?

2. What are the risks from not supporting Pat's requests?

3. What do you do? Why did you choose that course?

SITUATION 5-3
CAPITOL CANDY COMPANY

You are Mack Adamia and for the past 5 years have been an IS management consultant at Hy Stule and Associates, a regional CPA firm that offers management systems consulting in addition to its auditing services. Over that time your principle engagement has been with Capitol Candy Company, whose specialty is gourmet jelly beans, a continuing fad among the older Washingtonians. Many of their customers are prominent political figures and many are would-be politicians who buy and display your products in their homes. You have been very successful with CCC and have managed to gain the confidence of top management. Your recommendations have always been implemented and most have been successful. Unbeknown to the company management, you have really been making their IS management decisions under the guise of your consultant reports. They have become dependent on you to the point where their IS staff (including the manager) have become quite passive. You always seem to come through for them. You feel that the recent resignation of their IS manager, Hazel Knutz, may have been the logical outcome of that growing dependency.

The day after Hazel resigned you were called to the President's office. The President, Marsha Mallow, informed you of the resignation and the fact that it was no surprise. In fact, she said that Hazel had lost interest in her job, and despite their best efforts, they knew they were going to have to replace her. Marsha then surprised you by offering the position to you. She knew that you were quite happy at Hy Stule and it would take a pretty good package to turn your head. She offered you a 3 year (no cut) contract at nearly twice your current salary. Your major responsibility would be the development and implementation of a strategic planning process that integrated IS planning with corporate planning. A tall order considering the present state of affairs in the IS department. You feel compelled to take the offer for the money as well as the challenge but asked her for a few days to think it over before you answered. She agreed.

Your biggest concern is the level of planning to attempt. Marsha's request may not be achievable in 3 years, but you can work her around to a reasonable goal. At the same time you wonder about how much the IS staff and senior management can absorb. Too much will surely burn them out and lead to failure. Too little and the process will be ineffective.

1. How will you decide on the appropriate level of planning?

2. Outline your approach to implement the chosen planning system.

3. Is a fully integrated IS and corporate strategic planning process a good idea for Capitol Candy Company? Why?

4. Can you be more effective in implementing a planning process in you role as an outside consultant or in your role as IS manager?

six

□

The Organizational Placement of the Information Systems Department

SITUATION 6-1
BOILIN OIL, INC.

Boilin Oil, Inc. is a medium-sized refinery operation with wells located throughout Texas, Oklahoma, and Louisiana. They have just purchased a larger refinery operation in Alaska and have asked you, Hy Weigh, the IS manager to see what needs to be done to merge the two IS departments.

Boilin Oil has a tightly controlled centralized structure with all user departments tied to a single processor. All offices access the corporate mainframe from terminals at their desks. The sharing of applications and data across the organization are fairly common-place. Users have been kept satisfied even though they operate within a strict set of policies and procedures.

The Alaskan company, on the other hand, has a user community that has pretty much operated without the guidance and direction of a strong IS management team. Although the IS organizational structure is highly decentralized, it is nevertheless very progressive and has been able to use information technologies to great advantage in drilling and exploration activities. All the support staff have microcomputers on their desks as do virtually all professional and managerial personnel. The micros are networked and, except for sophisticated seismic data analysis, all computing activity is handled on the micro network. The company has been very profitable and owes much of that to the efficient and effective way that computers have been integrated into the organization.

As part of the acquisition, Boilin Oil agreed that the IS department of the Alaskan company would be retained. The current IS manager, Al Cann, now reports to Hy Weigh.

1. What considerations might you have as you decide on the best way to merge the two IS departments?

2. Under what conditions would centralization be the preferred structure?

3. Under what conditions would decentralization be the preferred structure?

4. If the two companies were located in the same city would it make a difference to your decision? Why?

5. Is there some other structure that could work better for you? Why?

6. What is your decision, and how will you implement it?

SITUATION 6-2
JACK NEIFT TRUCKING COMPANY

AT JACK NEIFT TRUCKING CO., OUTSIDE OF THE FINANCE FUNCTION, VERY LITTLE HAD BEEN DONE TO COMPUTERIZE.

Jack Neift Trucking has been a successful New England trucking operation for the past 30 years. It is still run by its founder Jack Neift, who is a workaholic if ever there was one. He has a number of direct reports and a penchant for getting involved in everything. Although many may criticize his management style, few can criticize the success he has had. The industry views him as a true entrepreneur. He is respected and at the same time feared by the competition.

Ever since you, Dusty Rhodes, joined the company, 6 years ago, you have been reporting to Hy Rowler, the CFO. He, like Jack, happens to be very demanding. But unlike Jack, he knows a lot about computers and how they can be used for competitive advantage in the trucking business. You have successfully implemented a number of exemplary systems for Hy and have a number still under development or planned for development. Outside of the finance function, very little has been done to computerize. You have a lot of ideas, but Hy has kept you too busy to think about anything but his requests. You sense some frustration on the part of the other senior managers, but they have chosen not to take on Hy.

The company is going to make a major move to computerize its truck routing system to significantly reduce operating costs and, hoped to be able to offer price cuts that will establish major barriers to the entry of new competition in New England. The plan is solid and is so important to the organization that Jack has you reporting directly to him until the project is complete.

1. How do you establish yourself at this new reporting level? What are the major issues as you adjust to reporting to Jack?

2. How will you deal with Hy? What about the other senior managers?

3. Outline your plan for meeting the continuing needs of company management.

SITUATION 6-3
BORUM-STRATE, INC.

Borum-Strate manufactures industrial and home drill presses that they sell through a network of 200 independent distributors located across the U.S. Owen Bucks is the CFO to whom you, Ann O'Dyze the IS manager, report. Owen hired you 5 years ago to develop a sophisticated cash-management system for the company. You accepted the position mostly on the fact that Owen was very computer-oriented, aggressive, and well-respected by the CEO. You and Owen have been a very successful team. The cash-management system was implemented ahead of schedule, and you are now working on a major forecasting system for capital equipment replacement.

Under the direction of Sid U. Ashun, the new CEO, a new corporate strategy has been approved by the Board of Directors. You participated fully in the development of that strategy, as it involves your department. As part of that corporate strategy, you now report to Sid. Sid has an excellent track record and has a reputation as a decisive decision-maker. Once the facts are analyzed, he moves quickly to a decision and to implementation. You are somewhat uneasy about the fact that his knowledge of computing is very weak.

A large part of sales come from the replacement parts business, which has recently been threatened by a foreign manufacturer, who is fully able to offer compatible parts below the price charged by Borum-Strate. Your task is to develop and install an on-line parts catalog showing exploded views of all drill presses in the product line and to offer your distributors on-line reordering from inventory. The foreign competitor will not be able to offer this level of service, and Sid feels that once Borum-Strate terminals are in the distributorships the threat from the foreign competition will be defused. The long-range plan is also to offer a variety of management reports to the distributors so that they can improve their own profitability. You helped develop the plan and feel that it is doable in the time-frame agreed on.

1. How do you deal with Owen now that you are his peer?

2. What do you expect in your new reporting relationship with Sid?

3. Do you feel a need to educate Sid? Explain.

4. Will you now take a more active role in priority setting? Why?

<hr>

SITUATION 6-4
SAN ANDREAS LAND DEVELOPMENT COMPANY

When your manager Rick Terscale, the Vice President of Finance, finally agreed with your proposal for the formation of a steering committee to assist you, Sue Nami, in IS planning and policy formation, hardware/software acquisition, application identification, system prioritization, and conflict resolution, you breathed a sigh of relief. At long last there would be a forum for serious consideration of IS issues. Life would be simpler for you, you thought, as you reread the memo announcing the formation of the steering committee.

For the first few meetings Rick, who chaired the committee, kept you busy briefing the members on the systems portfolio. You reported the status of every current as well as under-development system. There were often questions from steering committee members that usually required that you research the answers and report back at the next quarterly meeting or in writing to each member. The format repeated itself for the first year. You convinced yourself that this was simply the honeymoon and shakedown period. It would be over soon and the committee would get on with the work you had envisioned for them. In the meanwhile, the annual corporate plan was formed with little input from you. You recall asking Rick about changing the process to integrate corporate planning with IS planning. "We'll get to that after the steering committee is fully briefed on what we are now doing with the computer and our information systems," he quickly pointed out. You did not press the point.

At the last meeting you were to report on your response to the corporate plan. Of primary interest was the budget impact and development time lines for each of the requested systems. You have been experiencing significant declines in system response time for the last several quarters, and with the new systems that the plan calls for you are certain that the response time will be unacceptable. You reported your concern at today's steering committee meeting. Hugh G. Ruption, the Vice President of Research and Development and a heavy computer user, was quick to respond that the problem was not the processor capacity but rather the distribution of data across the disk drives. He further stated that he suspected the bottleneck was channel contention due to the excessive number or read/writes to the data base. With the data properly allocated to the drives, the channel problem would be alleviated and the current hardware system would adequately serve the company even with the new applications running. He sounded so convincing that Rich Tennant, the Manager of Contracts and Leases, asked if you could not do some further research on the channel problem and report back at the next meeting. He was quick to add that we need not be spending money on new hardware if it really was not needed. Rick concurred and without giving you a chance to respond, adjourned the meeting.

1. What is wrong here?

2. Describe the appropriate behavior for the steering committee at San Andreas.

3. What would you do to correct the problem?

seven

Information Systems Corporate Issues and Opportunities

SITUATION 7-1
KAMIKAZI AEROSPACE CORPORATION

Things have been going very well for you, Harry Kerry, the IS manager at Kamikazi Aerospace. The company has grown to capture market share in the private and small company aircraft business. Through your efforts, a number of strategic systems have been successfully implemented, the IS function is relatively stable, and the users are content. Your job has become somewhat routine, as you reported to the President, Crash dePlane (he earned the nickname Crash as a result of his less than heroic efforts as a Navy pilot in World War II) at your annual review last week. You also shared your interest in taking on more challenge. Crash agreed, and just this morning he offered to create the position of Chief Information Officer (CIO) and allow you to define the position and find your replacement. Rather than accept on the spot (and you were very tempted to do so), you asked for a few days to think it over. He was gracious enough to comply with your wishes.

You have identified four alternatives to consider:

1. Accept the position, find your replacement, and join Crash's staff.
2. Accept the position, find your replacement, but maintain your line responsibility with the new IS manager reporting to you.
3. Accept the position but do not replace yourself with a new IS manager (use the position elsewhere in the department).
4. Refuse the position, Crash is trying to buy you off, the company does not need a CIO and you need a new job.

1. What are the arguments for each alternative?

2. How will you decide which is best?

3. Would this be different in a larger or more sophisticated company? Why?

SITUATION 7-2

HI-TECH SASH & DOOR COMPANY

You are Izzy Able and have just recently joined Hi-Tech as their IS manager. Little did you realize the difficult position you put yourself into when you accepted the position. Wynn Dough hired you to replace him when he was promoted from IS manager to President. You were really impressed by that, as so few IS managers have ever been able to make such a move, especially in this industry. Wynn earned the position over the years by designing and installing a number of systems that effectively converted the business to a totally computer-based one. At the same time, the company moved from an industry laggard to an industry leader. Some claimed that it was through Wynn's efforts that this happened. Others were not so sure he deserved all the credit. All manufacturing processes were using sophisticated CNC machines and robots. Sales forecasts were continually updated with an algorithm that Wynn had personally designed and installed. The forecasts drove an MRP system that also included automatic purchase-order generation (another of Wynn's concoctions). The JIT features that Wynn installed had dramatically reduced raw material and in-process inventories. Customers were using an on-line order-entry system that included the ability to specify custom-designed products. Wynn was commended by the building and construction industry for this one-of-a-kind system. Shipping, truck dispatching and routing, and customer billing were also totally computer-driven. Wynn was almost single-handedly responsible for all these systems, and it would seem that his promotion by the Board was reward for having positioned Hi-Tech as the industry leader.

You, however, are quite different than Wynn. You hold a degree in Information Systems and an MBA from a prominent Boston-area business school. You have always prided yourself on the fact that you are a good manager and have a solid understanding of the relationship between IS and the business enterprise. When considering an IS decision, you always ask yourself if it is a good business decision. You are definitely business-driven rather than technology-driven. You expect to continue that philosophy at Hi-Tech.

During your first few weeks on the job you have had a chance to introduce yourself to the senior and middle level managers as well as the first-line supervisors. With few exceptions you discovered that Wynn had not been able to establish a trusting and cooperative relationship with them. Because of his superior command of operations research techniques and information systems, he totally overwhelmed the management team. "He's a super-techie, but left a lot of bodies on the roadside," was often used to describe him.

1. What kind of a president do you expect Wynn to be?

2. What strategies might you adopt in dealing with him?

3. Which is best? Why?

PART III

INFORMATION SYSTEMS AS A FUNCTIONAL ENTITY

eight

Duties of the Information Systems Department

▬▬▬

SITUATION 8-1
DAILY BREAD COMPANY

You are Willy Overbake, the IS manager for the Daily Bread Company, a bakery that serves supermarkets and outlets in New England. The company is privately owned by a very wealthy and involved family whose grandparents founded the business. Daily Bread has a 20% market share in the greater Boston area and feels that company growth will come in the form of new markets extending out 75 miles from their bakery in Cambridge and from specialty products that it can introduce in its Boston market and the newer outlying markets that it will establish. Although it is a medium-sized company now, its long range plan for new markets and new products includes a doubling within the next 5 years. You are a new member of the executive team and helped put the plan together. Your department is a major factor in the plan and will acquire bigger and better systems, hardware, staff, and budget. You are excited about your new role and the company's interest in using information technology. You believe that the plan is realistic and "do-able."

That is the good news, because you are also very uneasy about some of the planning assumptions that have been made. Your boss, Ginger Brett (the President and a member of the family), hired Clara Voyant, a marketing consultant, to do a few market forecasts that were presented during the planning sessions. The business plan that resulted was based on the conclusions in the consultant's report. The plan includes assumptions of a healthy economy; low inflation, increasing consumer spending, low interest rates, and low unemployment, healthy bakery suppliers, and so forth. You did not agree with the conclusions in the report; in fact, you see signs in the information systems industry that point to unstable and weakening vendor health, hiring trends, pricing, and so on. You also see this leading to future economic problems, including high unemployment, high interest rates, and desperate vendors. You also wonder if it would not be wise to plan for the worst. The more you have thought about it, however, the more you are not sure what the worst might be. You wonder if it will make any difference in the long run.

1. Are you going to follow Ginger's guidance or develop plans based on your own special circumstances?

2. If you do assume a bad economy, how will you proceed?

3. Are you going to explain your concerns to Ginger?

SITUATION 8-2
VIBRAGUM TOOTHBRUSH COMPANY

You are Les Plaque, the IS manager for the Vibragum Toothbrush Company, a small company that manufactures special-design tooth-brushes. For years Vibragum was a very stable, no growth organization that made only marginal investments in modern systems. Now, however, based on innovative new product introductions, the company has recently started to grow at an annualized rate of 30%. You are quite busy building new systems for marketing, manufacturing, distribution, administration, and others who recognize the need for their function to be supported by contemporary systems. You agree with the needs for the systems specified for these areas and feel that even though the IS department is very busy, that all systems will be successfully delivered on time thanks to your strategy of contracting out much of the programming.

Your only concern is for the general accounting department. They are using a batch general ledger system that is very old. It requires manual input from other systems and is thus error prone and labor intensive. Moreover, it requires substantial IS maintenance support to add edits, expand fields and tables, change the chart of accounts, and such. The problem is that the user is very happy with it. In passing, you once asked Ginger Vitis, the Manager of General Accounting, if a new, integrated, on-line system would not be appropriate. She responded that her department could not cost-justify the purchase or development of such a system. When you suggested that her department could actually reduce staff based on labor savings and that you could help with the cost justification based on the benefits of heavy maintenance avoidance, you were surprised by the answer. Ginger strongly disagreed that there were labor savings. In fact, she claimed that a new system would need more people to run it because her people were not very computer literate or good at working with new technologies. She pointed out that she did not have the time to make that kind of change within her department. Then she asked why you were pushing a new general ledger system. You said that you were not and that such a decision was up to her. Because general accounting is a key user, you wanted her to see IS as supportive and helpful. After all, she is ultimately responsible for getting the accounting work done and she should be allowed to decide how. Later, however, you had second thoughts. Company growth might require new reporting functionality and lead to transaction volumes that the current system would not easily handle. You are not sure whether Ginger is being conservative and cost conscious (the company still frowns on unnecessary spending) or if there is a fear or lack of understanding of technology. You are not even sure that you might be getting caught up in the excitement of all new systems and might be exaggerating the risks. The general ledger, though costly in terms of labor, is working well enough so far. Lastly, you are not sure what action to take. You do not want to precipitate a disaster but also do not want to let one develop passively.

1. Are you inclined to respond in a proactive or reactive way?

2. What would an appropriate reactive response be?

3. What would an appropriate proactive response be?

4. What circumstances might cause you to go to Ginger's boss to get direction? (Both of you report to the Vice President of Finance).

5. How might you test your opinions for possible prejudices?

6. How important is Ginger's support in committing to a new system? How important is the support of her subordinates?

SITUATION 8-3
PACK M. N. SARDINE COMPANY

You are Barry Cuda, the IS manager for the Pack M. N. Sardine Company, an aquaculture food products conglomerate that controls several different similar companies. Your strategy for each of the subsidiary companies has been to form a separate systems and programming staff that reports to you but is dedicated to that company. Technical support and operations are a unified shared activity.

Your company has just acquired the Fisher Cut Bait Company. It is a company without data-processing personnel or computerized systems. The strategy on acquisition was to treat them like the other Pack M. N. Companies and create a small systems and programming function for them and begin the automation process. Even though they are somewhat different from the other companies in how they produce and market their product, they are similar enough so that it is clear to top management that automation makes sense.

The person that you have selected to be the Manager of Systems and Programming for Fisher Cut Bait is a very experienced "fast track" project leader, Ann Chovy. She has several years successful experience at Pack M. N. Promoting from within is a company strategy, and you feel fortunate to have had a high-potential candidate like Ann. Unfortunately, you know that there are many skill areas that need to be supplemented. For example, all Ann's project experience has been on accounting projects and she has little experience in the important areas of marketing, distribution, and manufacturing. Moreover, if she and her staff are to tie Fisher's order entry, inventory, and other programs into the common company systems, she will have to learn a data-base management system and application code generator that she has not worked with before. Lastly, because she will have to build a staff, plan the activities, organize the work, direct the activity, control the quality, and more, you would like to see that she gets a chance to get some solid education in the area of management skills. You want to take charge of her development program personally. Naturally, as is typical, Fisher's management team is anxious to proceed with the automation program as soon as possible.

1. Prioritize the three types of education needed (technical, industrial, and managerial). Explain your rationale in picking this order. For which one, if any, would you schedule formal training for Ann in first?

2. How should Ann staff and organize her group?

3. What might you do to assist Ann temporarily until she gets her feet on the ground?

4. In retrospect, did you make a mistake promoting someone that needs as much training as Ann into an urgent situation?

5. Did you set her up to fail?

6. What alternative, other than promoting Ann to Systems and Programming Manager, might you have chosen? Why is this a good alternative?

SITUATION 8-4
DEWEY, CHEATUM, AND HOWE LAW FIRM

You are I.M. Honest, the IS manager for the law firm of Dewey, Cheatum, and Howe. You report to the Administrative Partner. Reporting to you are a systems and programming group, an operations group, a technical support group, and a training group. You have just implemented the results of a major effort to select a law department system. It consists of a word-processing system, document management system, docketing system, case management system, and a time and billing system all functioning on common hardware. It is purchased software that will be periodically updated but has been extensively modified by the systems and programming group to satisfy the precise needs of the users. All modifications were done under the direction of the vendor and will be incorporated in future releases of the product. Terminals have been installed for each lawyer, and for their secretaries, as well as in the word-processing pool. Training has been completed for all users, and everyone seems happy with the selection and implementation thus far. You, on the other hand, know that your worries have just begun.

Rather than the back-room, low priority department IS used to be, it is now in charge of a system on which the performance and profitability of the entire company depends. Senior management expects:

The system must always be available during working hours.

The system must perform quickly.

Data must be accurate and immediately available.

People must always be able to make the system do what they need (especially senior people).

People must be assisted around problems quickly.

The system must be kept modern with the latest functions and features.

People must be able eventually to move from simple tasks to complex ones.

The IS organization is aware of these service goals. You want to allow each group to be able to provide these services with a minimum of organizational coordination. In particular, you are trying to decide on where to locate a program maintenance group within the organization. It would be composed of people now within systems and programming. They could be left there and work with others who know the same skills and techniques. On the other hand, if they were part of operations they could coordinate systems access and focus on systems availability. As part of technical support they could concentrate on systems performance and the integrity of new modifications. It may even make sense to make them part of the training group because this group identifies needs for functional and performance improvements by working directly with users on a help-desk basis. You have also thought of making them an independent SWAT team so that no one concern would monopolize them. You do not expect to have any status or personality problems regardless of how you reassign this group. You just want to do whatever will make the system the most effective.

1. Identify the advantages and disadvantages of each of these alternatives.

2. How would you assign the maintenance group?

3. How would you manage the maintenance process?

4. How much personal involvement would you expect to have in ensuring a balanced use of the maintenance resource?

5. Have the expectations for the systems performance been set too high and preempted any chances that I. M. would have to balance his efforts?

6. Of the goals for the system, which ones seem most important?

SITUATION 8-5

HAIR TODAY SURGICAL REPLACEMENT CENTERS

You are Dan Druff, the IS manager for Hair Today Surgical Replacement Centers, a chain of cosmetic reconstruction centers catering to the tonsorial concerns of aging men. Your organization has experienced significant and profitable growth over the past several years, not insignificantly because of your efforts in identifying and implementing strategic systems opportunities in the services and the sales support areas. Consequentially, the executive management team considers you an important member of their group and plans to involve you more closely in future strategic activities. It is clear that, if anything, investments in technology will accelerate at Hair Today.

One of your recommended investments, which has been approved and is being worked on by your staff, is the installation of a LAN (local area network). It will tie together all of the company's personal computers, allow devices to be shared, permit a data-exchange program, and many other goodies that the users need. You are looking forward to its installation, so therefore you are not exactly delighted at the impasse that has been brought to you for resolution.

The selection of a LAN was to be preceded by a statement of requirements drafted by the project team. The team, headed by your Manager of the Information Center, Lou Gubrious, agreed that they would specify a preferred communication protocol. Unfortunately, Lou and the Manager of Technical Support, Mel N. Kolly, strongly favor opposite methods. Both are in your office now laying out their disagreement.

Mel claims that with his knowledge of technology he feels that CSMA/CD (carrier sensing multiple access with collision detection) is a superior technique and it should be chosen. Furthermore, he feels that it is more efficient capacitywise (especially for file transfers), more versatile, and is likely to become the popular choice of the future. Compatibility, he claims, will be important as the network grows. Lou cannot wait to disagree. He favors Token Ring as the right method. It has been chosen by the leading vendors, has the tendency for better responsiveness (less possible wait for interactive messages), and has several users right now. Lou believes that in the future it will not matter too much which technology you would have chosen in the past because protocol conversion will allow all networks to be integrated. As the meeting continues, each further justifies their own position with facts both significant and obscure. After laying out their differences, Lou and Mel ask you how they should proceed.

You are not sure that you fully understand or even agree with everything they have told you. You are more concerned that this decision be made in the right way than you are about the actual selection itself. If it is as fundamental as Mel and Lou suggest, then maybe you should educate yourself, get involved, and make a Solomon-like decision. On the other hand, this might be an issue that they should be able to handle without you. If so, you do not want to set the bad precedent of doing your staff's work for them. Moreover, it would be hard to back either one just in principle. Mel is responsible for all Hair Today technology and should have a say in the choice. At the same time, Lou is your project manager and your company has a tradition of giving leaders of projects the power to make important decisions, especially if they are to be held responsible for the efficiency of a technical solution. You are not sure what to do.

1. What role should the IS manager play in selecting technology?

2. Do you consider it good or bad that your managers are disagreeing and bringing the decision to you?

3. Could you ask both Mel and Lou to make a stronger, more objective and factual case for their opinion, as a way of enabling you to get the facts necessary to make a decision? What other tie-breaking methods might you consider?

4. How appropriate would it be for you to force them to work together until they reached a mutual agreement? What risks would that entail?

5. Are Mel and Lou arguing over the right things? If you had to make the decision, what criteria would you use to make a choice?

6. What action would you take?

nine

The Elements of Information Systems Department Management

SITUATION 9-1
PIGGE BANK COMPANY

You are Nick Uldime, the IS manager for the Pigge Bank Company, a medium-size regional bank that has been heavily investing in computer equipment and technology but has a long way to go before its application systems are as effective as the bank would like. As a result of the recent corporate planning process, the need for a comprehensive customer information system was identified. Your boss Flo Dallone, the bank president, would like to propose this project to the board of directors and gain their support for immediate project initiation. Because you are not a large bank and because the board is very active, Flo warns you that they will be very interested in the details. Although you have a pretty good knowledge of the banks systems, you know that the person on your staff who is appointed project manager will have to be strong and assertive. You have such a person in mind; Dee Posit, a senior member of your systems and programming department. Dee is currently busy completing the final stage of a major project to convert your current customer systems to a new data-base structure. Her boss, Anne Newitease, is your systems and programming manager and has strong skills in sophisticated customer information systems for banks. However, she has only been on board for 1 month and does not know your bank's systems and is still not well known. No one on your staff has participated in the bank planning process. They are busily performing the aforementioned technical migrations. Flo says she would like you to outline what you feel the board should hear, remembering that we want to get their approval for a spending plan that would complete this system.

1. What are some of the components you would include in your plans for this project?

2. What pieces can and should wait for later?

3. Who do you involve from your staff?

4. Who do you involve from the user community? How are they involved?

5. Do you have any recommendations for the president about who should present this to the board, when it should be presented, how much detail and scope should be offered, and so forth?

SITUATION 9-2
OCTOPOD INDUSTRIES

Chris Tullball is the IS manager for Octopod Industries, a large and growing industrial concern that has eight subsidiaries that Chris provides with information services. A few have their own operations groups and IS liaison functions, but the rest of the activities are her responsibility. Her organization is fairly typical, with a systems and programming manager, a technical support manager, an operations manager and an internal services manager (library services, training, quality assurance, etc.) reporting to her. Recently, Chris and this group have spent an increasing amount of time on company planning. In addition to an extensive IS plan document, Chris makes frequent submission of project plans and revisions to these, budget recommendations and revisions, financing recommendations, project status reports, user meetings and communications to coordinate her plans, and many other related activities.

She is beginning to wonder if it would not be more efficient to move some or all of this function off into a special function. She would like to see this whole area get more detailed and knowledgeable attention without becoming a burden on her or her staff.

1. What action would you recommend she take?

2. Should a department of IS planning be created?

3. Should such a unit be a senior position with power to make planning decisions or a clerical function that gets all input from others? Where should it report?

4. Assuming one person would start out in such a function, what skills and background should that person have? Would it be better to get someone from within the organization or look outside?

5. What are the advantages and disadvantages of the various alternatives?

6. What arguments might you advance for doing nothing?

SITUATION 9-3
TRY & BUY DEPARTMENT STORES

THE DEPARTMENT KNEW THE COMPANY WAS DOING THE RIGHT THING, ONLY NOW THEY DID NOT FEEL A PART OF IT.

You are I. M. Emprest and have just been hired as the new IS manager of Try & Buy Department Stores, a retail marketing chain. You were specifically hired to update the IS department by installing a data-base management system that the company knows they need to control multistore inventory, central ordering, vendor management, pricing, spoilage, and a number of other areas. In fact, this is right up your alley. You have been involved with similar projects in other companies but never as IS manager. The company has given you a free hand and the users you have met are more than willing to defer to your ideas. Your department, on the other hand, feels betrayed by management. They are all company veterans who slaved for years in obscurity and neglect. They are all generally very capable. For the last several years they have made similar recommendations to management only to be turned down and asked to "keep the company running with what you have." Now they feel that their loyalty and good ideas have been rewarded with an outsider being brought in to implement a "top management program" that by now has become critical. They know the company is finally doing the right thing, only now they do not feel a part of it. Moreover they recognize that you have more skills in this area then they do and are intimidated by it. They promise to work with you and to support you but are disappointed with the way the company chose to implement what they like to think of as "their idea." You have a major project in front of you, and it is critical that you do not alienate or further demoralize the staff.

1. How do you organize the project? Do you serve as the project manager or do you appoint someone from within the department?

SITUATION 9-4
ANTHEMUM & DENDRUM WHOLESALE FLORAL SUPPLY

Chris Anthemum and Rhoda Dendrum are the founders and owners of the worlds largest and most successful wholesale floral supply company. Their success is heralded in print and on television. They have more than 200 warehouse locations throughout the United States from which they supply approximately 11,000 retail florist shops. You are Bea Gonia, the Vice President of IS for Anthemum and Dendrum, and have remote IS operations at each of the warehouses. Each location has its own local IS function, which reports to the local general manager but with dotted line responsibilities to you. You must approve their annual budget, their IS plan, and any major technical project they may propose. Each business is very similar in terms of size, product produced, and so forth. Likewise, each uses similar technologies, though there are clear differences from location to location in applications run, software used, procedures followed, and other features. You believe that all IS professionals could benefit from stronger ties to you and each other. Both you and your boss Chris believe that this would in turn strengthen the business. Up until now local IS professionals have dealt almost exclusively at the local level. You believe that improved communications will be the best way to proceed since trying to work through the planning process or by your directive is too heavy handed.

1. What communication methods would you choose?

2. Who would you single out for communications; the local data processing head, all technical professionals, all managers in the IS function, all IS employees?

3. What would be the nature of communications sharing—top-down education/direction, sharing experience by each location, joint planning, and so forth?

4. How important is physical location to some or all of your communication?

5. How much of your time and their time would it be appropriate to devote to this project annually?

SITUATION 9-5
BORE

You are Theo Congame, the IS manager at a large government IS department of the Bureau of Revenue Enhancement (BORE). Your department has recently been funded to develop a major system for taxpayer reporting. Without going into detail, this system would keep historical records on tax payments and send a letter to taxpayers annually on historic payments and estimated upcoming tax base. The system is supposed to pay for itself in reduced or earlier taxpayer queries, earlier tax bill payments, and improved relations. It is, however, a multiyear effort with several design problems to overcome, such as how to keep up with taxpayer relocation, what exactly to tell taxpayers, how to accumulate history from various sources. The project is a very visible one. Even though it is being designed with the tax department as the user, other peers, such as the finance officer, are very interested in it. Moreover, a board of public officials, one of whom is your boss, Dee Laze, is anxious to make political hay from this system. As is the case in public administration, there is open and marked disagreement about the system. However, you and a strong project manager reporting to you have been given complete latitude to design the system as the process tells you, free from political influence. Still, you know that the controls you place on the process and the visibility of these controls will make a great deal of difference in the acceptability of the system. Furthermore, you are concerned that the multiyear nature of this project makes the regular budget controls inadequate.

1. What are the various controls that you see as being needed?

2. With what controls do you personally want to be involved?

3. What controls do you want users to have?

4. What controls should the board of public officials have?

5. Should you or your project manager play a stronger role in dealing with public officials?

6. How often should they get involved?

ten

Functional Challenges and the Information Systems Manager

SITUATION 10-1
THE HINDENBERG GAS COMPANY

You are Pete Bogg, the IS manager of the Hindenberg Gas Company, a regional utility providing service to more than 10 million locations. As with many large monopolies, your company suffers from a reputation for poor customer service and weak community relations. One of the things that contributed to this in the past was an ancient billing system. Because of it, customer bills were usually late, wrong, or missing. There is little information available to customer-service representatives about current bills and no history information whatsoever.

The good news is that your department is funded to replace the system for the billing department, and everyone is very excited. The bad news is that everyone wants something very different from the project. Capp deFumes, your systems and programming manager, sees the opportunity to expand his department with many of the group technicians taking the long-awaited step into a supervisory role. The users have a long list of traditional detailed requirements and, having waited for years, are not prepared to accept any compromises. The very influential Vice President of Public Relations, Shirley U. Jest, and the President, Dick Tator, want something very soon to put the ground swell of customer complaints and attendant nonpayment into remission. They feel that it could even be temporary, as long as it is quick, it does not have to be perfect. The Vice President of Finance, Amanda B. Reconwith (the likely next president, but not directly in charge of billing) on the other hand, believes that a high technology, sophisticated state of the art system is the way to go. Not only would it generate positive customer relations and favorable press, but it would last for a long time. Everyone knows based on experience that this system will have to last for a long time.

Your opinion will very likely decide the issue. You do know that Capp, although very new and inexperienced, has already made up his mind and is strongly in agreement with his staff that the project should become a large in-house construction effort. Moreover, they would like to take a stab at some of Amanda's ideas for new technology. You do know that a decision on direction needs to be made and the project started.

1. What approach are you inclined to favor? Why? Assuming a system with 80% of the features was available, would you buy it?

How much do political factors, business factors, or technical factors enter into your decision?

2. If you have no strong convictions, how would you go about making up your mind?

3. How would you go about presenting your decision? What methods might you use to promote consensus?

4. What risks might the eventual project run?

SITUATION 10-2
COCK AND BULL STEAK HOUSE

You are Phil A. Mignon, the IS manager for the Cock and Bull Steak House, a chain of some 100 company owned restaurants that is growing at the rate of 15% a year. As IS manager you are responsible for home-office computing, mostly accounting systems, central purchasing systems, and inventory systems that are very old. The computer on which they run is very old as well, but it is working adequately. Unfortunately, your growth has made the existing system inadequate for current needs. An upgrade is needed immediately.

You and your department have narrowed the choices down to two very different alternatives. The first is the easiest; acquire the latest and next bigger model (almost twice as big and costing $500,000) from your current vendor. Although this will support all current programs and would be simple to convert to, it has some drawbacks. The technology is still not very advanced. It will not support some features that your company will want soon, such as interactive point-of-sales systems, interface to food co-op buying system, and decision support tools. Furthermore, it is unclear if your vendor, who is known as "Old Reliable" in the business, will ever get them. They are not known as pioneers. They are known for superior inexpensive support and training to which you can attest. You have never had a service complaint and have used their training extensively. If you go with this system, it will be the biggest offered by your vendor, although they have always added to the high end of their line.

The other choice is a vendor who is a pioneer. Their system is equal in speed and cost to your vendor's system, but it is in the middle of a full range of computers offered by this vendor. They are smaller than "Old Reliable" but are growing faster. Their rapid growth has meant that they have occasionally dropped the ball in servicing new accounts, and their technology is so new that there usually is no formal training for a while. The computer you have tentatively selected has many advanced features that you would not get by upgrading with your current vendor including decision support systems and communications interface. They do not currently have interactive point-of-sales systems but promise to have it in 9 months. Their reputation is that they always deliver new functions on time, though it may take some time to get all the bugs out. The biggest obstacle to selecting this system would be the conversion of existing programs to work on the new system. You know that some functions, a few important ones, can never be converted. An outside consulting firm will do as much as can be done in one big effort for $300,000. You have also looked at having your staff do the work all in-house, though this would take 6 months if everyone worked at it full time. Changing vendors has many implications, mostly negative in your opinion. Your people are trained in the skills of your current vendor and you know it would be easier to hire more of the same skills than to get employees knowledgeable in the new vendor's technology. On the other hand, you are not so sure that your staff would not find it more professionally rewarding to go with a more progressive vendor. Both vendors are lobbying aggressively for the business.

1. Which vendor would you recommend? Why?
2. Are there any other strategies that should be considered?
3. What are the most important considerations in your decision?
4. What risks would each approach invite?
5. Should this be an IS call or should top management make the decision?
6. Under each strategy, what would a good acquisition approach be?
7. How much should the IS professionals be involved in this decision?

SITUATION 10-3

EXTENDED CREDIT AUTHORIZATION COMPANY

You are Val E. Date, the IS manager of the Extended Credit Authorization Company. Your company is a medium-sized company in the business of authorizing credit card transactions. Firms accepting credit cards as payment either call, use on-line facilities, or batch their transactions to you where you check your data-bases for credit worthiness before authorizing or disapproving the transaction. You then track the credit balance of all customers until updated by the billing authority. Yours is a growing business with on-line facilities located across the United States in 5 locations. Obviously, systems availability, data accuracy, program control, security, compatibility of technology, and technical improvements are all important factors that you must provide for your company.

Your Manager of Technical Support, Kurt Remarque, comes to you with a request for more personnel resources. You are sympathetic to Kurt because he has only 3 other people in his department; a systems programmer, a data-base administrator, and a communications analyst. With the company's recent growth, you do not see any problem getting one more position authorized. The big question is what kind of a position should it be. Kurt is no help because he goes off on a tangent naming dozens of areas where help could be used. These include:

Security coordinator
On-line systems administrator

System library manager (program libraries, etc.)
Technology researcher/coordinator
System change tester
User (client) training

There are others as well. You know that to get approval you will
have to be specific about the necessary job.

1. What other positions might be appropriate?

2. Given the circumstances, what position would you establish for
the additional person? Why?

3. Where would this position report?

4. Should Kurt be more responsible for this decision? Who else
should have a say in the decision?

SITUATION 10-4
O'NEILL & PREIGH CHURCH EQUIPMENT
MANUFACTURERS

You are Sal Vation, the Vice President of IS for O'Neill & Preigh, one of the largest manufacturers of church furnishings and equipment. They sell both stock and custom-designed furnishings to churches all over the world and are listed among the Fortune 500 companies. Their products are among the highest quality in the industry, and O'Neill & Preigh are recognized as the industry leaders.

You and the Vice President of Manufacturing, Ben E. Dictus, both report to the President, Del E. Lamma, a sales-oriented high-level manager. You and Ben are good friends (as well as neighbors) and both agree that the time is right to begin to automate the manufacturing process. Right now you are in a growth curve and can afford it. In the inevitable downturns, you are looking to automation to reduce the direct cost of production and give you a price edge over the many other small competitors.

Beyond this goal, the agreement between you and Ben stops. You believe that Ben has not let your department do enough for him in conventional systems such as MRP and inventory control. There is an order-entry and fulfillment system and a purchasing and receiving system, so manufacturing does work with computerization today. You think CIM is a nice goal but should be planned out and implemented in the right order. You feel that your technical staff should help Ben's staff put such a plan together.

Ben is much more impulsive. He thinks that most conventional systems and planning activities will delay getting to the real "diamonds" (to use Ben's term). He thinks that a few isolated systems such as a laser-scanning system to detect joint tolerance and a bar-code tracking system to instantly locate customer orders, will give high payback in a short amount of time with little people involvement. He believes that you are unintentionally creating an empire and pushing some of your favored employees into positions of challenge. On the other hand, you know that Ben is responding to some degree to one of his foremen who has been lobbying for more automation for a long time.

You believe that Ben's "diamonds" are by and large good opportunities. However, you think that manufacturing may be guilty of oversimplification to think that the benefits come simply by plugging in technology. Time is short and money is not inexhaustible. Budgets are to be set in 2 weeks. If you both budget differently or in duplication, Del will get involved and settle the issue. Neither of you want this, as Del does not like disagreement on his staff and deals with it ruthlessly. On the other hand, if you and Ben can agree on a strategy, approval is almost guaranteed.

1. What action do you take to reach an agreement?

2. How much can you personally afford to compromise before giving in to Ben's wishes? How important are his wishes? Would you want him to give in completely to you?

3. What are some of the responsibilities for which you would argue the hardest?

4. What are the biggest risks of following Ben's plan? What are the biggest risks of following your plan?

5. What players need to be involved in determining the strategy and to what degree?

SITUATION 10-5
B. STOVEBURDEN MOVING AND TRANSIT COMPANY

You are Dee Livery, the IS manager of the B. Stoveburden Moving & Transit Company, a privately owned medium-sized regional moving company. Dee has just been approached by a subordinate, Rick Shaw, Manager of Quality Assurance with a problem. He has determined that the software testing process is not thorough enough and he would like to take responsibility for all final application testing rather than just review the test procedures as he does now. You are somewhat sympathetic because several systems have been recently implemented with embarrassing and costly flaws. Moreover, the internal audit staff has criticized the testing process as being ill defined. The problem is that Laurie Driver, the Manager of Systems and Programming, strongly disagrees.

Laurie recognizes that there has been unsatisfactory testing. However, she maintains that it is mostly caused by (1) unclear user specifications and lazy user acceptance and (2) the tremendous management pressure to implement projects quickly. She further believes that Rick doing the testing will be counter productive. First, it will slow down project productivity that is already being criticized. The systems and programming professionals would not like to be directed by Rick, as they would have to be during final testing. Lastly, Laurie believes that Rick's lack of intimacy with the new system, both technically and applicationwise, would cause him to do a worse job than systems and programming could. Laurie urges you to not approve Rick's request but address her own concerns. You know she has to do something.

1. Would you support Rick or Laurie? Which one? Why? If neither one, why and what would you do?

2. Are there other approaches to fixing the problem?

3. What other information might you want in order to make a decision? How should you go about getting it?

4. Might there be more to either Rick or Laurie's story than meets the eye?

5. What other issues should you consider in making your decision?

6. How should you implement your decision?

eleven

□

Organizing the Information Systems Department

SITUATION 11-1
QUILLEN, INC.

You are Otto Graff the new IS manager of Quillen, Inc., a manufacturer of fine writing equipment. On taking over the department, you are surprised at one interesting characteristic of your new technical support department. With more than 12 technical professionals, all hold the identical title of systems programmer. You find this is a realistic reflection of the fact that everyone works on a similar variety of technical support tasks. In your previous company, a technical support department of a similar nature provided specialized titles of operating-systems programmer, telecommunications analyst, data-base specialist, and technical-support consultant. Moreover, each of these titles had a regular and senior level to reflect a professional's advanced skills. Both your old company and Quillen have similarly sophisticated data-base and telecommunication networks, as well as significant roles in assisting systems and programming.

You came from an environment where you considered the technical support job structure too specialized. Now you are dealing with a structure that at first glance may be too simplified. You are not sure how to proceed.

1. What evidence would you look for to discover if a problem exists in the technical support department at Quillen?

2. How might the job structure have stayed so simplified during the sophistication of Quillen's technical environment?

3. What dangers would too specialized a job structure cause?

4. What risks do you run in changing the structure? How might you go about it?

5. Of the two extremes, which should you err toward at Quillen; too generalized or too specialized?

SITUATION 11-2
UDDERLY DELICIOUS DAIRY COMPANY

You are Carry dePail, the IS manager for the Udderly Delicious Dairy Company, a producer and marketer of dairy products. You report to the president of Udderly Delicious along with the Vice Presidents of Marketing and Sales, Product Development, Manufacturing, Distribution, Finance, and Personnel. That is until this morning. In a surprise announcement, the president shared his intentions to reorganize the company along product lines. Marketing and Sales, Product Development, Distribution, and Manufacturing will be divided into 4 integrated groups, each focusing on one of the major product categories:

1. Whole Milk Products Group
2. Milk Solids Products Group
3. Frozen Milk Dessert and Confection Products Group
4. Milk By-products Group

The current vice presidents of the functional line units will be assigned to head one each of the new product groups. The president solicits everyone's ideas on how best to implement and support it. After a spirited discussion of mainstream issues, the issue of support comes up. The president emphasizes that IS, Personnel, and Finance will continue to report to him but asks each support executive how they intend to react organizationally to the new structure. Personnel says that they would probably not change but continue to provide central services with the same structure. Finance on the other hand says that they would probably divide their analysis and transaction-processing groups into 4 similar units so that their support people could specialize in serving one product group. When you are asked, you admit that you are undecided. The president asks you to sleep on it and give him a preliminary indication in a day or so.

Currently, you have a mainframe computer that is managed by a single operations department and supported by a small technical support department. Your systems and programming department is organized by function, with a separate group supporting each of the old organizational units. The systems they build and maintain are capable of distinguishing among product groups now so the systems can support the new organization. However, you know that requests for conflicting modification to existing systems, especially marketing systems, are inevitable. You frankly do not know how to proceed. In critical functions like distribution, you know you do not have enough good people to assign one to each product group. Moreover, you know that with 4 groups making uncoordinated changes to the applications, the systems will tend to become unstable. Yet the president has made it clear that good IS service to each product group is extremely important. Currently, vice presidents are used to having a team that is highly knowledgeable about and dedicated to their systems. You are not sure you can provide both.

1. Why might you feel that both systems knowledge and dedication from systems and programming will be hard to provide?

2. What disadvantages might you encounter in functional groupings by product line? What merits does it have?

3. How could the current organization still support the new structure?

4. What are some of the various methods of providing product group focus, addressing maintenance, control, operations, technical support, and so forth?

5. Is there any merit to waiting before evaluating a possible reorganization? How much should the wishes of the new product group heads be considered?

6. Based on the available information, what are you inclined to do?

SITUATION 11-3
GEPETTO'S TOY SHOP, INC.

You are Jack N. deBaux, the IS manager of Gepetto's Toy Shop, Inc., a very large manufacturer and distributor of children's toys and games. As a key member of a very competitive industry, you constantly have several major systems projects underway simultaneously and in recognition of the importance of this effort have organized systems and programming in a task-oriented function.

Thus systems and programming has 4 major groups, one each on three major projects and one to handle maintenance. This has worked fine for every task except maintenance. Not surprisingly, it has turned out to be the group no one wants to be in. Competition is keen to get out and into one of the "good" (major project) groups. Maintenance consequentially has a very poor reputation. Even the talented people in maintenance are perceived as having low ambition (or bad sense) or else why wouldn't they get out?

Although some of this is normal reaction by systems and programming professionals to a less than glamorous task, you feel that it has been carried too far. People are not staying in the function long enough to gain the necessary skills and are not intent on learning the systems well enough to become proficient at maintenance. The maintenance requests that receive the most attention are the newer systems where the maintenance analyst/programmers can try to impress the major project teams who are still slightly involved. These new systems do seem to receive more than their share of support. The really rickety systems where help is really needed are too old to have a major project team member connection and therefore do not receive the urgent attention that they deserve. You are intimately familiar with the problem because your Operations Manager, Ted D. Baer, has complained at length about the problems it is causing him. Important reports have been delayed for days owing to systems that cannot be fixed expeditiously. Worse, repairs have occasionally been made improperly, resulting in delivery of erroneous data or loss of critical systems for days. You know that action is required.

Resorting to management attention (alternately cajoling and threatening) once again does not seem like it will be any more effective than it was in the past when these problems occurred. Lou Neetune, your Manager of Systems and Programming has attempted to strengthen his team but it just will not stay strong. Moreover, Lou has his key objectives in the progress on major projects. You and Lou cannot afford to focus on maintenance in any way that will detract from the all important major projects. Also laying the problem on Bea B. Gunn, the Group Leader responsible for maintenance, does not seem right. Bea is the only member of the team that is highly capable and available at all hours to fix problems. She is an outspoken critic of the attitude that treats maintenance as a second priority. You feel that she tries hard to build an effective team, but every time that a major project job becomes available, her best people seem to wind up being selected through the company's hire from within program. Maintenance ends up hiring from outside because no one wants to go there, and the cycle repeats itself.

This time you think something fundamental is required. You are prepared to move the maintenance team under Ted and try to divorce its activities from the major projects. Before you make up your mind, you want to review the pro's and con's of such a change.

1. What advantages would such a realignment bring? Would it help to address the subject problems or would they continue?

2. What disadvantages would it perhaps cause?

3. Is reorganization too drastic a solution? What other actions should be considered?

4. How would Bea react to working for Ted? How would Lou react to losing Bea?

5. What action would you take?

6. How would you go about implementing these actions?

SITUATION 11-4
ST. ELMO'S FIRE ALARMS, INC.

You are R. Sonist, the IS manager at St. Elmo's Fire Alarms, Inc., a growing manufacturer and marketer of fire alarms, smoke detectors, heat sensors, and sprinkler control systems for the consumer and industrial market. Your company has facilities in Flaming Gorge, Wyoming; Volcano, California; Burning Tree Estates, Maryland; Hot Springs, Arkansas; Fire Island, New York; and Devil's Lake, South Dakota. More facilities are planned soon. Between company growth and normal growth of technical opportunities, you have your hands full of projects.

Your main concern is for your Technical Support Manager, Blaise N. Flame. As you have grown, Blaise has naturally picked up responsibilities for voice communications networking, end-user computing software, personal computer support for users, programmer productivity software, and some automated manufacturing technologies. Although Blaise is very competent at directing her 6 subordinate technicians in the technical side of her responsibilities, you are seeing indications that attendant areas are not being properly addressed. User-support processes are consistently found wanting, as is any planning or preparatory activity. The company's activities cannot stand second-class treatment much longer.

You have just finished confronting Blaise with your concerns. She feels that she could do more planning and develop better user training and request processes if you would only give her additional staff. She may be right. However, you increased her staff by one person last year and things did not get better. (She responded that one person is not enough.) You are also worried that regardless of how many people Blaise has, she will always hire technical people like herself who will always put the technical component of their job at the highest priority. You are afraid that Blaise may be subconsciously avoiding tasks that she does not like (or do well).

If you are correct, there are several courses of action you can consider. First is the radical step of replacing Blaise with someone who has broader management skills. This may not be a popular step because she is known to be a loyal employee and a sound technical professional. Another approach is to start reducing technical support's duties. One way would be to spin off new functions. An information center could be established to handle end-user computing issues or an office automation group could be set up to deal with voice communication and other functions. You see where they could be better focused, but you worry about losing the strategic synergies and strong technical coverage. It is possible that they could report to Blaise but if she is contributing to the bad situation this would exacerbate the problem. Another way to reduce technical support duties would be through reassignment. Some duties could be given to systems and programming or the data center, but this would be a clear loss of face for Blaise. Moreover, those groups are busy too, and if the problem is having the appropriate skills then systems and programming and the data center may have the same problems as Blaise. A final approach would be to not change the organization at all but to help Blaise address the deficient areas through some directed training, consulting help, and personal help from you. However, you do not have much time and you would have to strongly believe that the necessary skills are quickly learnable and that Blaise can learn them.

1. Which approach are you inclined to favor? Why?

2. How much does the choice of a decision depend on Blaise's skills and abilities? How much should be done simply as sound organizational practice?

3. Are you managing the technical support properly? Are you adequately managing Blaise?

4. Are you making organizational decisions in the correct context? How should such a decision be made? What other factors should be taken into consideration?

twelve

☐

Information Systems Personnel Management

SITUATION 12-1
HUMBLE SHEPHERD CHURCH HEADQUARTERS

You are Hal E. Lewya, the IS manager for the Humble Shepherd Church headquarters. The organization is a large and growing apostolic religious order and as such has a sizable data-processing organization to support the systems it requires, including accounting, personnel, pension operations, fund raising, trust funds, securities management, loan operations, and real estate activities. You pride yourself in that you run a very effective and well thought of operation. You are naturally alert to any behavior that you feel may suggest future problems. Just such a problem, you feel, may be surfacing itself in the behavior of Pearl E. Gates, one of your project managers.

Pearl has been working on the new foreign currency arbitraging-system project. (Despite their higher calling, Humble Shepherd is also very practical.) The work is going well but Pearl's behavior has you worried. She has begun increasingly to work nights and generally to isolate herself from everything but her technical duties. On days when she is in the office, she seems to avoid contact with users and managers even more than usual but keeps her nose to the grindstone doing technical work. Her rare breaks tend to be spent with a few technical support people "talking shop." You and Pearl have always been friends, so it is easy for you to share your suggestion that she spend more time with the users and the rest of the IS department. You point out that if she could be "more human" that she would be a more effective project leader.

Pearl is bemused by your comments and quickly makes a point-by-point rebuttal. She says that she gets along very well with all her users without being "buddy-buddy" with them. "Being a social butterfly is a matter of personal style and not a job requirement for project leader," she says. "Talking with key department experts makes me more technically skilled. As for working alone in odd hours, you would not be so pleased if I spent more time communicating because the work would not get done." You counter by saying that your suggested adjustments are subtle but nonetheless appropriate and should be carried out over time in order to make her a better project leader. She disagrees and feels it would make her a less effective performer because it would be counter to her personality. "If it ain't broke, don't fix it," she concludes. In reviewing your conversation you wonder who is right.

1. How much diversity can a user-interface job such as project leader tolerate?

2. Will the environment and job structure allow Pearl to change? Can her behavior be easily modified?

3. Might Pearl's behavior have other less profound causes?

4. Should Pearl try to become more extroverted?

SITUATION 12-2
REST ASSURED BEDDING COMPANY

You are Robin DeCraydull, the IS manager for the Rest Assured Bedding Company, a manufacturer of bedding and bedroom furniture products. Your department is a sizable company activity, but as with all Rest Assured operations, you run a very lean operation. Management has been pleased with your past focus on cost containment and increased efficiency.

Everyone in the department has accepted this strategy with the exception of the newly hired technical support manager, Matt Tress. Matt was hired based on his strong mastery of the company technology, his familiarity with the industry, and his record of solid technical achievements. You have not regretted the hire, as Matt is a hard worker and has made several significant improvements that have won him the respect of the IS staff. The only problem that you have with his eagerness is that he is adamant that each of his ideas be carried out.

The latest and most serious blowup has just occurred. Matt came to you claiming that more DASD (direct-access storage devices) must be purchased. He agrees with you when you point out that storage capacity is far from being exceeded, but he insists that unless the data are not quickly spread out over more access area that serious performance problems could result. Matt further points out that if they wait until the problem occurs (as you suggest), it will be too late to respond properly. You thank Matt for his observations but confess that, knowing the facts as you do, you feel the risks are small enough and the cost of DASD great enough to postpone this purchase. You are surprised when Matt gets upset. He accuses you of not doing your job by not informing the top management committee of this serious risk. He respectfully suggests that you are just a management "hatchet-person" with the responsibility to contain costs with no thought to the consequences. After informing you that he plans to appeal in writing directly to the President, Lou Quarm, he leaves you wondering how you might have avoided this confrontation.

You would like to retrieve the situation for several reasons. First, you would like to establish a relationship of cooperation not confrontation with Matt. Second, you would like Matt, like all IS department members, to share in the reason that certain decisions are made at Rest Assured. Furthermore, of some concern to you, is to shield Matt from a possible run in with the President, Lou Quarm. Lou is a nice guy but he does not like problems and if he has to deal with them, definitely does not like dissent. In the face of the two, Lou has been known to be very high handed and tactless. You do not mind Matt dealing with Lou although you do not look forward to calming Lou down. You are more worried with Matt's ability to deal with Lou.

1. Is this a simple disagreement over a business issue or are their elements of personality differences at the bottom? If so, do you feel that these personality differences are linked to the role of IS professional or manager?

2. How might you have dealt differently with Matt? Are you dismissing his concern too quickly?

3. Do you think Matt is a good fit for Rest Assured? Will he be a good employee in Lou's mind?

SITUATION 12-3
WHOLE CLOTH MANUFACTURING COMPANY

You are Ray Ahn, the IS manager for the Whole Cloth Manufacturing Company, a small producer of fabric for the garment industry. Your company is marginally profitable and survives thanks to the most parsimonious and rigorous of management styles. As a result of this, your IS department only undertakes the most vital of projects.

As a further example of organizational leanness, there are no full-time managers reporting to you but instead several operational and technical professionals plus two project leaders. One of these project leaders, the chief programmer Polly Ester Pantz, is the cause of a certain degree of frustration. She and her assistant analyst are close to completion of a new invoicing system that will save a lot a money by ending the need to hand-write customer invoices. Until it is finished, Whole Cloth is paying 3 temporary employees to perform the tedious, error-prone work.

The president, Terry Towl, who is your boss, is impatient for the system to be completed as soon as possible. You have relayed this strong request to Polly along with your observation that you think she could be proceeding more quickly. You even offer to get her temporary help, which she refuses as inappropriate. The project is already past due, but as the due date was arbitrarily imposed by Terry, you do not find that too incriminating. What you do find disturbing is that Polly seems to be over designing. She is laying out a "watertight" system with a lot of consideration for future expansion, extensive audit controls, restartability, and run efficiency features. You tell her that you do not think she appreciates the need for urgency.

She counters that you are a typical executive that does not appreciate the complexities of computer systems. She points out that if she "crashed in the slipshod system that you wanted," it would fail, with substantial cost to the company in manual labor, customer problems, and most of all, her time plugging the holes. While you acknowledge that you do not want that to happen, you suggest that a better balance of speed and features could nevertheless be struck. Polly disagrees. She claims that she is in the best position to determine the right balance of all important project features and that she is already doing it. She will not commit or even guess at a new completion date until her design has been completed and approved by users because she believes that it would come back to haunt her. With that she storms out of your office vowing to "continue to do it right."

You do not know what to do. You have the skills (though not necessarily the time) to take over the project personally and design it following Terry's and your conceptions. That is the last thing you want to do, most of all because Polly is the real expert on this application. But Terry claims that he can not keep paying for temporary help indefinitely. He wants answers and action.

1. Is Polly displaying a personality trait typical of technicians or sound professional judgment?

2. Can and should such attitudes be changed? If so, how?

3. What is the IS manager's role in such an executive/IS professional impasse?

4. How do you answer Polly's assertions? How would you deal with her?

5. What do you tell Terry?

SITUATION 12-4
HAPPY LANDINGS SKYDIVING SCHOOLS

You are O. O. Oops, the IS manager of the Happy Landings Skydiving Schools, a chain of schools specializing in teaching people various ways to fall out of airplanes. Your firm is very broad-minded and has expanded into several other related areas: skydiving clubs, skydiving holiday tours, skydiving competitions. You have even started marketing your own merchandise, such as your line of designer parachutes (Motto: Good to the last drop.). This has meant that your IS group is always rushing to put in new systems to support some new management program.

Your people are good and enjoy their work. However, you have just been presented with a complaint from your systems and programming staff for the first time in years. Phyllis Stein, one of two senior project leaders, has visited you to object to your "prejudicial treatment" of one of the systems and programming staff. She claims that all of systems and programming, whom she was chosen to represent, are offended by the special consideration you afford Earnest F. Fort. You have never assigned Earnest to a group project but have always given him projects that he could work on alone. This looks like more fun and more glory to others in systems and programming. You are never pressuring Earnest to meet with users more as you are doing with the rest of the department. Consequently, he can work nights and weekends without being tied down to week-time user conferences. The biggest objection is your practice of asking to be involved in everyone's general design sessions to contribute your ideas but exempting Earnest. You accept his designs without much change at all, but feel you can add your ideas to those of the others. Phyllis concludes by saying that "We want fair treatment, and that means consistent treatment."

You say that you are sorry to hear that everyone feels that way because you believe that you treat everyone fairly. In your mind this does not imply in consistency because you treat people differently based on their differing skills. You try to assign independent projects that require little user interaction to Earnest because he works best that way. He does not have strong user relation skills. Others do. Moreover, Earnest does not function well with close management involvement, so you give him some room. The rest of systems and programming performs very effectively when working closely with you and, except for the resentment of Earnest, does not seem to mind it. You close by telling Phyllis that all this does not make Earnest a better or even a more specialized employee that he is just different and you believe that everyone should be treated so as to make them most effective. You remind Phyllis that many on her team need your constant encouragement, although you do not "stroke" others, even Earnest that way.

Phyllis is not satisfied. She accepts what you say about treating everyone individually, but claims this should not extend to preferential treatment. "Earnest", she states, "gets better assignments and better working conditions just because you think he works better that way. Who wouldn't?"

1. How do you answer Phyllis? Is she right?

2. Should all employees be treated alike? What would happen to Earnest if he were subjected to generic treatment? What might happen to the rest of systems and programming if the current practice is continued?

3. How would others respond to the treatment Earnest has been receiving?

SITUATION 12-5
ST. METHUSELAH HOSPITAL

You are Anne Gyna, the IS manager for St. Methuselah Hospital a privately owned 600-bed hospital and clinic. The hospital has a number of money-making activities, such as laboratory services, that must all be supported by your IS systems. New money-making ventures are an important part of St. Methuselah's strategy. A temporary revenue shortfall at the hospital has determined the climate for the last year and a half during which strict cost controls have been required. In response, you have had to undertake new projects with your existing staff and cut corners wherever possible. One such opportunity has just been presented to you. As a further needed source of income the hospital administrator, Cole Kompress, who is your boss, wants to provide more comprehensive patient billing and collection services for area doctors. From a project standpoint there are a lot of dimensions to this effort. It means having to work with the resident doctor's committee to find out their needs as well as insurance representatives to meet their requirements. It also means tieing into existing hospital accounting systems for current patient billing in addition to the construction of a whole new accounting system for this business service. The latter includes a system to charge the doctors for this service.

Fortunately, you have two skilled project leaders (independent analyst/programmer types), each with skills in this area. Ivy Tube has been with the hospital only a year but already knows the current patient tracking and billing system very well. Moreover, she has impressed all your users with her eagerness, constructive communication skills, and business orientation. She is a good planner, too. Then there is Hy Podermic. Hy is a fixture at the hospital with close to 20 years of service. He wrote most of the accounting systems that are running today, including the very complex insurance rebilling and collection system and the general ledger system. Although not well liked by your users, Hy is the senior statesman of the IS department and is respected for his broad applications knowledge, his technical skills, and his "lightening like" coding prowess.

The problem you face is that this project is probably a two-person effort and together Ivy and Hy have the right talents. But two more different people you cannot imagine. Ivy relishes communicating whether by meeting or memo; Hy hates it and simply does not do it. On the other hand, Hy is famous for his heroic crash systems implementations that have more than once rescued the hospital from problems. Ivy is more a "work to rule" person when it comes to doing the actual technical work and is not noted for speed or high degrees of accuracy. Hy is much older and more experienced than Ivy, but Ivy is more ambitious and is clearly aware of her talents. Lastly, Ivy is good at following orders and working cooperatively with other. Hy, on the other hand, has earned his bad reputation by being argumentative, opinionated, and contradictory. In his defense, Hy is often "right" and is always raising salient concerns or problems even when others do not want to hear them. However, you sometimes wonder if he does not go out of his way to irritate his user counterparts. Unfortunately you do not know how Hy and Ivy will work together because they have never had that opportunity. Socially they are pleasant enough and, although they do not have much in common, they fraternize with one another occasionally.

You know the project needs two people. You could tap some other member of your staff, but no one else brings any particular skills to this effort and may be of no help at all. Projects have always had someone in charge, but you are wondering if you need to appoint one project manager. Or maybe you should artificially make two projects out of this. You do not know. The only thing you know is that Cole needs this system as soon as possible.

1. Will Hy's and Ivy's different styles conflict or will the diversity complement each other? How important is that on a temporary project?

2. What bearing does the leadership status of either one of them have compared to their ability to work together on a peer basis?

3. Which one might you imagine has the more crucial skills for this particular project?

4. What particular action would you take? How is this influenced by your perception of the two personalities?

SITUATION 12-6
NEW CLEAR WASTE DISPOSAL COMPANY

You are Ray D. Ashun, the IS manager of the New Clear Waste Disposal Company, a firm that removes, handles, and gets rid of certain objectional materials. In compliance with the mandates of federal, state, and municipal regulations, you are improving the controls and protections of the systems operation. One action you have taken is to create the job of data center programmer. This new position would report to the operations manager and be available to respond to systems failures, make emergency changes to programs, improve performance efficiency, and so forth. This would improve system performance considerably; you have experienced two or three program-related failures each week as well as other problems and inefficiencies that could be avoided with the attention of a good programmer. Because some of the problems are of a technical nature, you have written the job to state that systems-programming experience is highly desirable.

You are in the process of sketching out a newspaper ad for the personnel department to place in the local paper when your senior computer operator, Helen A. Handcart, drops by to see you. She tells you that she has heard rumors of the new job and wants to be considered for it. You know that Helen has recently finished her programming training at a local night school and was waiting for an opening in systems and programming to develop so that she could apply. You had not thought of Helen for the job because you were thinking of someone more senior. This person would work pretty independently and would not get much technical help from their boss, the operations manager. (Helen reports to the operations manager in her current position.) You explained this to Helen, but she feels that she can do the job, learning what little else she needs to know along the way. Systems programming, you pointed out, is not easily learned on your own. She responds that she works well with the current systems programmer and a phone relationship is all that is really needed anyway. Besides, Helen points out, what she may not know about technology she makes up for with her extensive knowledge, built through 8 straight years in the computer room, of New Clear's applications and their idiosyncracies. You are well aware of Helen's knowledge and skills and have been dreading the day when you would lose her as your senior computer operator. However, to lose her from the company would be far worse. Although she is not your first choice for what you had in mind for seniority and experience of the data center programmer, you could give her the job in the hopes she will grow into your requirements. You also could change the job content to fit Helen a little better and assure that she was successful. Or you could tell Helen that this job is not for her and that she should wait for the right job to come along.

1. What factors should be important to you in order to make your decision?

2. Are there any possible compromise solutions that could better satisfy the needs of all parties?

3. What action would you take? How would you justify it?

SITUATION 12-7
LOTTA BARX DOG FOOD COMPANY

You are Scott Terrier, the IS manager of the Lotta Barx Dog Food Company. The company makes, packages, and distributes pet food products throughout the United States and Canada. The data-processing operation has been recently called on to perform above and beyond the call of duty. In response to a big sales drop, a new distributor quota allocation and sales tracking system was needed fast. You were happy to report to Doc Sund, the President, that in the short interval of 2 months one of his senior systems analysts, Kay Neincorr, and many consultants were able successfully to design, code, test, and convert to a new system. It seems to be working well 1 week later. Sales have not responded yet, but everyone is hopeful.

Your current concern is with Kay. She performed magnificently and you feel is deserving of some special recognition. Not only did she accomplish this successfully, within budget, but did so through long hours away from her family, rescuing acceptable agreements from dangerously firm user opposition, introducing calm and objectivity into panic-stricken, stress-dominated conditions, adding ingenuity and creativity to an otherwise stalled project, and generally championing its success. You helped in more than one tense situation, but feel that the bulk of the glory goes to Kay. Indeed, you believe that if something positive is not done soon, you may lose Kay, if not to termination, at least to the grip of bitterness and resentment. She is well aware that her performance is extraordinary and in her exhausted and burned out condition is looking for some kind of organizational support. Because the eyes of the rest of the department are on this situation, you want to respond with a meaningful and appropriate reward.

You believe that to emphasize the significance of Kay's achievement, the reward should come from the highest company level and be something tangible. Things you are considering include a gift certificate, cash bonus, a promotion to a newly created more senior position, extra vacation, courtesy trips to carefully selected distributor sites, and/or visible recognition, such as a write up in the company newsletter, lunch with the President, or special citation. You are also considering assigning her to an upcoming major project that promises to be even more important, but at the present time this might be seen as a slap in the face.

You have met with Doc and Ray Beese, the Vice President of Personnel, to discuss the right action. Doc is willing to do something, but Ray warns against doing too much. He warns that since sales have not yet gone up we do not want to give an employee cash or such to celebrate something that could be a failure. Moreover, he feels that a promotion is not the right way to respond to a one-time success. Ray agrees that Kay's performance is deserving of recognition, however, he believes that to be too generous would set a bad precedent for others in the company who do fine jobs every day. Doc asked you to respond to Ray's concerns.

1. Do you agree with Ray's opinions? How do you answer Ray's remarks?

2. If Doc should give you carte blanc, what reward(s) would you choose?

3. How do you rationalize the success of Kay's work with the uncertainty over the effectiveness of the system?

4. Are you making too much over the issue of Kay's reward? Isn't it reasonable to expect senior IS professionals to be understanding about the timing and degree of rewards? Shouldn't the reward you control be enough for Kay?

SITUATION 12-8
STICK TIGHT FLYPAPER COMPANY

You are Anne Teeter, the IS manager for the Stick Tight Flypaper Company, a medium-sized manufacturer and marketer of insect-destroying products. You support the company's data-processing needs with a small IS department that includes a 10-person operations department, a 3-person technical support staff, a 12-person systems and programming department and one secretary. Also reporting to you is the Senior Technical Analyst, Aaron Buoy. Aaron is a highly skillful technician who has contributed to many of Stick Tight's most innovative applications of technology. Unfortunately, he has always sought greener pastures whenever he gets bored, which is frequently. He is ever anxious to earn increased status and rewards to which he feels his vast talent and contributions entitle him. You recognize Aaron as one of the great minds in the company.

Unfortunately, the combination of his irascible nature, his unwillingness to work for anyone else, and his genuine senior contributions have earned him a place on your staff. There he is kind of a technical ambassador without portfolio, working on important projects that the both of you agree on.

Aaron has just come into your office, closed the door, and announced that he is once again tired of his job. However, this time he makes an interesting admission. He says he is ready to become a manager. Aaron claims that he can advance no further under the current organization structure without taking on supervisory duties. So he feels that must be his next step. Frankly, he wants to be your replacement. Therefore to get ready for it, he proposes that you split up systems and programming, leave half with the current systems and programming manager, and give the other half (all of whom are his junior) to Aaron to get some important major projects done. When you ask Aaron if he really looks forward to being a manager, he says he does, that he has always seen himself leading an IS department. Even though he admits that he has never supervised others he believes that he can learn the skills required. He points out that he already has the intelligence, the business understanding and the technical skills to be the IS manager. You thank Aaron for his interest and tell him you need to think about it.

The decision facing you has many facets. You know that Aaron would be an insensitive and an intolerant boss. But he is capable enough to get things done. Besides, where else can he develop supervisory skills? Aaron's recommendation would not be a popular move, especially with the systems and programming manager and Aaron's new staff. Particularly unpopular would be any suggestion that Aaron is your potential successor. No one on your current staff is seen as having a shot at the job should you leave nor practically would they expect it. Although all respect Aaron, they know that he has only professional tolerance for them. At the same time, you are not sure you believe that Aaron wants to be a manager. He enjoys technical problems to the exclusion of all others. However you are not sure a small shop like yours can support a high-level technical job to which you could promote Aaron. You know, however, Aaron would be much happier working for the president, free to practice technology with a free hand. Nor can you think of a good alternative job available or one that you could create to give Aaron as a distraction. The remaining alternative, do nothing, is not a good one. Aaron's request will soon turn to insistence and possibly his resignation. You do not want to lose Aaron. He knows too much about your existing technology and promises to be crucial to the next round of technical innovations. But you are stuck for a good answer.

1. Are there alternatives that should be considered that you have overlooked?

2. What risks would you run with Aaron as a manager? Do you feel his commitment to be a successful manager would cause him to learn the skills?

3. What risks do you run by disappointing Aaron?

4. What career path would you recommend for Aaron? How would you explain this to Aaron?

thirteen

□

Information Systems Development Methodologies and Projects

SITUATION 13-1
ESTER'S PERFUME COMPANY

You are Dee O'Durant, the IS manager for Ester's Perfume Company, a medium-sized manufacturer and marketer of feminine cosmetics and fragrances. Your company has grown smoothly and successfully using systems that where 100% developed by your in-house staff using traditional technology, tried and true but fundamentally sound. The development of these systems were guided by an in-house system development methodology that very thoroughly and very specifically told them how to construct new systems components. Your staff follows these rules precisely and in fact relies on them. You are pleased that the whole systems-development life cycle works so efficiently and that the IS department has the sweet smell of success.

Unfortunately, a fly has just landed in the ointment. A project with a preliminary budget and time frame has just been approved for a new accounts payable system. Under normal procedures, your project manager, Terry Daktul, would meet with users to determine a complete statement of needs. Once the users agree that this is what they want, an adjusted time estimate/cost estimate is presented to management for approval. With the go ahead, Terry would then assemble a team to do the work and complete the project, including testing, training, documentation, and so forth. However, Ida Clair, the manager in charge of accounts payable, has complicated matters by strongly suggesting that purchased packages be evaluated. Although she has no particular package in mind, she wants something that can be implemented as soon as possible and with more features then Ester's can usually afford to build. You and Terry have no objection to a purchased package but are concerned with the process of evaluating and acquiring one. Terry strongly feels that an independent requirements statement is needed before looking at packages. Ida wants to start looking now. (Terry accuses her of wanting to go "window-shopping.") Terry has also raised the need for an outside package to conform to all internal development standards, such as naming conventions, and documentation standards. If a package is selected, he claims to need time to understand it before making a sound estimate of effort to install. Ida has expressed her concern that "IS is just looking for an unimportant excuse to either avoid purchasing a package or making a big project out of modifying one."

Beside your efforts to keep harmony between Terry and Ida, you are worried that top management's role needs to be modified. In a way, this should have been considered earlier as the money budgeted for this project was assumed to be the use of IS staff time and no out of pocket cash was set aside. (You do not want to lay off IS people to free up expense money.) Moreover, the project expense was spread over two budget years, not the single period expense that a package purchase would entail. Management will also want to know about issues of consistency should a package be acquired. Other previously defined roles such as functional training and maintenance, would have to be redefined. In short, this departure causes IS some real problems. You are not sure how to proceed.

1. Should you recommend handling this project as a special exception, should you use your systems development process as closely as possible, or should you take the time to modify it to better accommodate packages? Might you even need a separate process entirely for purchased software?

2. Should you and Terry work with Ida to develop one recommendation and take that to top management? Would you build two
options (one make, one buy) and let management decide, or would
you ask for their philosophical direction now?

3. Are you and Terry really unbiased? What are the pros and cons for
your systems and programming staff of purchased software?

4. How do you think requirements should be developed, look at many
packages and compare, independently state existing needs and
wants, or some combination? What are the disadvantages of each
approach?

5. What are the disadvantages of making a make versus buy decision
too early in the process? What are the disadvantages in making the
decision too late?

SITUATION 13-2
FREE LUNCH PARTY HEADQUARTERS

You are Al B. Tross, the IS manager for the headquarters operation
of the Free Lunch Party, a political organization that believes in ad
valorem taxes, the platinum standard, the adoption of "Yankee
Doodle" as the national anthem, and widespread distribution of
baloney sandwiches. Your field organization is attracting a growing
throng of voters to your party to support these and other important
causes.

You and your group are in the final stages of developing a new
party-member tracking system. Through it all fund-raising is conducted, all opinion sampling is done, and all contact sheets are
provided to your field operatives. It replaces an archaic version of the
same thing with many new features and information options. Most
important of all, it is on-line and is the only way that the small Free
Lunch staff can handle the anticipated heavy volume. Obviously, it
is a critical system, but based on the extensive travel and nonavaila-
bility of your key users to give you all specifications and to review
designs, you are not sure that conversion will go as smoothly as
everyone hopes. You raise your concerns about the correctness of the
new system. This surprises everyone because they thought you had
the project under control. When you suggest a postponement of
conversion, everyone shudders at the thought and says that it

cannot be done. The presidential elections are just 6 months away. Between now and then are the prime times for fund-raising, new member recruitment, member involvement, and so on. Because another key opportunity will not come for another 4 years, there is some urgency to get the system installed. It is not an issue of if but how.

You are meeting with key figures to decide what to do. The membership manager, Frank D. Bate, wants the system yesterday. He votes to install the system ASAP, fix it as we go along if necessary, and back out if too painful. The Marketing Manager, Jerry Mander, who is in charge of fund-raising, wants a clean system. Any back out would mean that all his contact lists would have to be regenerated and all his collection data manually converted or he would be asking people for money twice. He is in favor of a parallel system so that he is assured of accurate continuing marketing programs. The Political Action Manager, Vito Powers, who runs the opinion analysis program, strongly objects. He does not have the staff to handle double the work. Moreover, he can afford to wait a month or two until the software is tested out. He wants to test out several sophisticated elements that require situations that do not come up routinely. Others, like Jerry, believe that only real-live data will prove to him that it works correctly. The Party National Chairperson, Polly Tichen, everyone's boss, asks if the system could be used only for new members for a time. Frank likes it, but Vito and Jerry roar at the thought of the work it would cause them.

Polly then asks you for a few facts. You claim that setting up a parallel system would take a month and cause some operational confusion and risk. A pilot program can be set up more quickly, but this does not include getting any "real" computer data to it for testing. The back out could return us back to the old system, but most data recorded in the new system would have to be reentered, something no one is staffed to do, and much of it would be lost as the old system has no place for it. When Polly asks whose preference carries more weight, an argument ensues among Frank, Jerry, and Vito that their needs for the new system will help the party more. During this Polly pulls you aside and asks you what you recommend now that you have heard all the facts.

1. Assuming you were aware of this evolving problem, how might you have gotten user and management attention and headed it off?

2. Which method is the most attractive from a purely IS standpoint?

3. How do you factor the alternative levels of risk and business needs into a decision-making process?

4. Who should make this decision, and how should it be made?

5. If your recommendation is the deciding one, what would you do?

SITUATION 13-3
PEACEFUL PRODUCTS MORTUARY SERVICES

You are Barry DeBones, the IS manager for the Peaceful Products Mortuary Services Company, a division of William Randolph Hearse Industries. The company is a producer, marketer, and distributor of products to the nations mortuaries and funeral parlors. Business is predictable and reliable, so your department benefits from a stable development environment. The IS department implements about two new systems a year, which are usually improved replacements for existing applications. In addition, the technical support group usually introduces two or three new software versions annually, all in a very controlled way. In short, the relative predictability and stability of the IS environment would be the envy of other IS managers.

Ever anxious to strive for perfection, you are trying to eliminate a nagging problem that has consistently caused the only noticeable problem. The maintenance team, headed by the IS maintenance supervisor Doug deGrave, is always running to catch up with problems. As new systems are implemented, his team has no real knowledge of them up to the point that the first problem occurs and maintenance is called. Then they must quickly figure out what is going on in order to correct the problem. In such a situation, they find it frustrating that the documentation is often not to their liking, the application structure sometimes unnecessarily complex, and the programs awkwardly written. Similarly, new software releases cause like problems because problem correction must sometimes be done differently as technology changes. Consequently, the maintenance team has always had a low opinion of the new project staff's and technical support's ability to be efficient and pragmatic, not to mention their willingness to communicate.

Doug's solution to the problem is straightforward. He wants maintenance to have approval over everything that goes into production. Maintenance would conduct thorough testing, review documentation, inspect code, and actually perform the implementation of acceptable software. Things that did not meet their specifications would go back for repairs. Doug contends that he could afford to do all this with the time his group would save from reduced maintenance. Cleaner systems would be better for the users, and he would be taking testing and implementation work off the shoulders of new product development and technical support.

The New Projects Manager, Paul Bearer, is not so sure. Paul feels that this extra "sign off" will add delay to projects and frustration for his staff. "How," he asks, "do we know what will satisfy maintenance anyway? They don't even know now until something breaks. Besides, if they had their way we would never put in anything new." The Technical Support Manager, Anita Wake, agrees. "Maintenance may know about preventing work for themselves later on down the road, but they don't know the first thing about things we pay attention to in our tests and implementation, things like functionality, performance, back out."

You know that Doug is not imagining his problem, and he knows more should be done to head off problems. However, he does not want to create new problems and is worried by the warnings of Paul and Anita that inefficiency and mistakes might result.

1. What are some of the risks to making the changes Doug suggests?

2. Can such a new process be tested or experimented with?

3. Is a major process change too strong an action? What lesser measures might be tried?

4. What would you do and why?

SITUATION 13-4
CLOTHES LINE NEWSPAPER

You are Phil dePage, the Project Manager for the Clothes Line Newspaper, Inc., a holding company specializing in trade publications for the fashion industry. The project you are responsible for is the design and installation of a personnel package to be used by the human resources department for the management of the approximately 450 full and part-time employees of the company. Management and the user department have approved this project based on your estimate of 1.5 man years and 6 months to completion. You anticipated about 6 people involved, some full-time. You know that the 6 months to implementation was especially important in gaining management support because it would allow the system to be implemented January 1, the beginning of your fiscal year. Because it is now April 15th (what better time to think of a personnel system), you think you have plenty of leeway.

Now that the project is underway, the feedback of several of the team members throws doubt on this implementation date. One person in particular, Benny Fitzpackage, the assigned programmer, has turned in estimates for his pieces that double the estimates you made initially and would push the implementation date out over 1 year from now. You feel that your estimates are reasonable and attribute the "padding" in Benny's figures to bad experiences that the IS department has had in the past with missed schedules. When you set up a meeting with Benny to go over his estimates, he shows up in a very adversarial mood. He states he will not work under a schedule that he does not believe in and will not be put in "another pressure cooker with management imposed deadlines." You decide not to argue with Benny for now. You spend about 20 minutes going over his calculation, disputing nothing, and thank him for his time. He leaves you the impression that he still expects you to try to hammer down his numbers.

You realize that this is only one approach. Obviously, you could go to management and ask for a postponement. You have no idea how they would react. You could also spin off some system functionality into a phase II project. This would permit some of the more important features to be implemented this year but would delay others into next year. Users will not like this but may accept it if they think the alternative is a cancelled project. Finally, you know you could negotiate with Benny and probably reach an agreement that would just get the project in under the wire. Unfortunately, this would not allow any fallback for legitimate delays. Furthermore, you know that Benny (as most other people) will work to the schedule and not try to better it. You only wish you could convince Benny that with a reasonable and honest effort your original time estimates are correct. You assume that Benny could do the work within this time but does not want to take the risk of what he thinks are aggressive schedules.

1. How important are the motives behind how people estimate work load? Is it not all the same to the project regardless of their reasons?

2. What systems of incentives might improve the situation?

3. How much control does the project manager have over team-member productivity?

4. What approach should you take with Benny to determine the final work schedule?

5. Which course of action would you take?

SITUATION 13-5
KOPH AND KNALES TOBACCO COMPANY

You are C. Garr, the Project Manager for the market research system project of the Koph and Knales Tobacco Company. Your company is a very old firm but has recently entered into the very profitable specialties tobacco market with such products as your breath-freshening pipe tobacco, vitamin-enriched cigars, smokeless cigarettes, and cigarettes with pastel smoke. In order to assess the potential markets for these and other new products correctly, top management has asked you to put together a proposal for a system that will track sales and be based on various coupon programs, point of sales surveys, outlets results, ad campaigns, and general demographics. The President, Winston C. Garets (better known as "Smokey"), is particularly anxious to get a state-of-the-art system partly owing to the increased revenue opportunities and partly for the extra prestige it would give him within your industry. This is one of those projects where money is no object but time is of the essence.

You have spent many hours with Nick O'Teen, the head of the research department. Nick has an ill-defined idea of the system he would eventually work with as being a sophisticated collection of every management science tool known to man. This conflicts with your interpretation of what Smokey needs; which is a vast data repository of sales results for analysis by multiple variables. This difference of perception does not worry you as much as your concern over the scale of the project. Koph and Knales has never gone in for sophisticated analysis, automated or otherwise. You believe that the ability for your company to absorb a lot of complex systems success- fully all at once is limited. Nick does have the help of an outside industry expert, Chester Fields. Chester supports the idea of pro- ceeding full-speed ahead, but you see this as a case of a vested interest.

Were it left to you, you would start small and phase in the features over time. You clearly believe that this would at least get several easy benefits implemented soon. However, you are worried that if pre- sented this way, with most of the major benefits admittedly post- poned for a time, Smokey would lose interest or look for some other way to get this kind of research—such as contract it out. Another approach is to hire someone with more sophisticated research experience into Nick's group. You know that Nick would oppose this proposal as an insult to his and his staff's talent. If the only course of action is to commit to a highly sophisticated system, you wonder if you have all the skills necessary for the challenge. Perhaps an assistant with experience in selling systems to users and a major training background would be advisable. Perhaps the downside risk is not so very great after all, and you should proceed along the most optimistic lines.

1. How much does risk assessment play in making a directional decision? Is this the role of the project manager?

2. Shouldn't you just present the options and your recommenda- tions to Smokey or Nick and let them decide?

3. What other options should be considered?

4. What course of action would you recommend?

fourteen

□

Information Systems as a Functional Entity: Issues and Opportunities

SITUATION 14-1
JADED PALATE PAINT COMPANY

You are Manny Hughes, the IS manager of the Jaded Palate Paint Company, a manufacturer of private-brand paints and spirit-based decorating products. Your company is growing and expanding every day as part of its long-term strategy, but in such a competitive industry you are very expense conscious. Right now you are faced with the unpleasant requirement of upgrading your mainframe computer because your growth has caused normal transaction volumes to exceed your existing capacity.

You are fortunate (though this might be debated) to have two clear choices that will run your existing software with no modifications. The first is an old-type machine in the same family as the one now in use. It would be purchased on the open market used. The other choice is a new technology machine. The machines have the same capacity and rated speed (twice what you have right now), though expected enhancements to the new machine promise further improvements. The old style machine is one-fourth the price of the new machine. (Both are cheaper than the price you paid for your existing computer 4 years ago.) The new technology is not expected to be replaced for another 5 years because this seems to be your vendor's cycle of improvement.

You believe that the newer technology is the right investment. It will avoid expensive maintenance later on, you could sell it for not too much less than you bought it for, and in the mean time you could benefit from the ever-improving performance. Your boss, Red Dye II, the company president, is not necessarily in agreement. Red is tempted by the low cost of the old technology and feels that so much extra capacity could not be consumed in 5 years. You counter argue that the price may be lower but the net devaluation on the two systems will be about the same if you sell the new technology before its price drops precipitously. Until then, depreciation on the newer machine offers more assistance to cash flow. Moreover, you suggest that there are many hidden costs of inefficiency on the older machine. However, putting yourself in Red's shoes, you realize that there are arguments both ways.

1. What other facts would assist you in making this decision?

2. What would you be inclined to do? Why?

3. Is too much being made of the asset issues? If so, how would leasing help?

SITUATION 14-2
NOTEWORTHY MUSIC COMPANY

After a month on the job, you have identified some differing but strong attitudes on the part of some key executives.

You are Vic Trolla, the newly appointed IS manager of the Noteworthy Music Company, a medium-sized manufacturer and distributor of music-related products: musical instruments, sheet music, music equipment and supplies, and such. The company is pressured to control spending by some recent lean years. However, if the past flat revenue streams are to be "ramped up," then everyone knows that selective, high leverage investments must be made.

The IS department has not been very successful in recent years, hence the sudden departure of your predecessor. An increasing work load precipitated some real support problems. All major work is identified and authorized by the executive management committee with all minor work requested by users and authorized and prioritized by the IS manager according to rules based on ROI. In the past, the increasing critical work piled up while scarce resources floundered with rapidly maturing requests. You were hired with a minimum expectation of improving this frustrating situation.

You have set as your own objective for the IS department to maximize the benefits they provide to Noteworthy. After a month on the job, you have identified some differing but strong attitudes on the part of some key executives. The Chief Financial Officer, Al Toesaks, is your boss. Al sees your key job as controlling IS expenses for the entire company as well as providing accurate data management. The President, Mel Otious, is inclined to view you as a service center. As long as you support sales, manufacturing, distribution, and so on and keep them happy, the president feels that you are doing a fine job. Your Manager of Systems and Programming, Bertha D. Blues, believes that IS's contribution is measured in terms of the number of new things that IS does given the traditional scarce resources. Many functional executives seem to think that your first duty is to keep production systems running reliably.

1. Are these various views by Bertha, Al, Mel, and others at odds with your objective?

2. Is there any danger in such a diverse set of opinions?

3. How might you go about changing attitudes if required?

SITUATION 14-3
SLIPPERY GRIDDLE BRAND FATS AND OILS

You are Shirley U. Slidemoore, the IS manager for the Slippery Griddle Company, a vendor of brand name and private branded vegetable oils and edible fats for cooking. The company is a stable but profitable medium-sized company that has a tradition of taking good care of its employees but being very tight with discretionary dollars. Your job over the last few years has been to improve the performance of the white-collar environment, and you have installed several well-received tools to do just that. The President, Chris Coe, your boss, has given you a reasonably free hand in this endeavor.

All has gone smoothly until just a minute ago in Chris's weekly staff meeting. When asked about the effects the new tools have had, you described the voice store and forward system, the electronic mail system, the graphics system, and the group document-sharing system that has been installed on a trial basis. You further explained that because the IS professionals now conveniently do much of their typing, distribution, filing, document preparation, meeting arrangements, and other tasks, the IS department secretary, Lindsey Doyle, has been mostly freed up to perform IS department studies such as budget analysis. In response to a bombshell of a question from Chris, you stated that other employees could also undertake much of the same functions and eliminate the need for the company's heavy reliance on administrative support. Although some agreed, several others at the meeting showed open and strong opposition to such an idea. You tried not to precipitate things, but the fat was in the fire.

Castor Hoyle, the Vice President of Marketing, was the most adamantly opposed. He admitted that because all such services are voluntarily available within the company, many of his employees use some of these tools now. However, he does not encourage this owing to his beliefs that "We pay secretaries to type and managers to think!" Castor feels that his department must use existing secretaries and the services of the administrative department to be allowed to concentrate on their own chosen specialties. Even though you related the opinion of your department that administration was better—faster, more direct, more extensive—using the tools, he does not agree. "Having a secretary is seen as a benefit by many of my managers," Castor argued, "and they would get upset if they lost the dedicated help of these administrators. If these tools mean that we will lose either our secretaries or administrative department support, I will order my department to discontinue using any of them."

May Zolla, the head of administration, said that even though everyone knows Lindsey likes the fact that she is no longer being everyone's servant and that she is challenged by the more responsible work, the employees in the general services typing pool, the mail room, the telephone operator (who takes all phone messages), all see themselves as professionals in their own area and would not like to see some of their duties go elsewhere. May also believed that the quality of the work would suffer when done by amateurs; typing would be sloppy, recorded voice messages are unprofessional, and so forth.

Chris listened patiently and did not take sides. As the cross fire died down, he made a number of points. "Although it may have been nice to let the use of these tools evolve, now that battle lines are drawn it may be necessary to decide now which way we plan to go. First," he said, "no one will lose their jobs. We have a lot of work like the kind that Lindsey undertook and much flexibility of assignment in that. Secondly, we cannot afford to do it both ways too much. Some secretaries will always be around and a few tools may always justify themselves. However, the tools are too expensive not to get wide use and I believe that two ways could cause employee resentment and envy both ways. Most importantly, I do not just want to do what is most popular. I want to go in a direction that will really improve the performance of this company." Everyone agreed to objectively look at all the issues, collect more first-hand facts, and meet in a week to discuss it. Chris said he would make the "policy part" of this decision, and all agreed that they would abide by it.

1. What are the pros and cons of each fundamental direction?

2. What are the critical factors that will determine this decision?

3. Is it reasonable to expect everyone to work one way?

4. In hindsight, should you have answered so conclusively?

5. How do you think Chris should decide?

·Part IV·

INFORMATION SYSTEMS AS A USER SUPPORT ENTITY

fifteen

The Role of Information Systems as a User Support Entity

SITUATION 15-1
MERLIN PHARMACEUTICS (A)

Merlin Pharmaceutics is a manufacturer of a wide range of prescription and over-the-counter drugs. Their products carry their own labels and are distributed directly through their own sales force, which operates out of eight regions in their U.S. and Canadian markets. They do not compete in any international markets. They have performed at the industry average and are known as a conservative company. The Board believes that their "slow but steady" philosophy coupled with their very deliberate management style has given their customers the perception that they are a stable and reliable company, and the same goes for their products. Customers have a high degree of confidence in the Merlin label and are not likely to switch to a competitor brand.

You are Anne T. Dote, the IS manager. You have learned to operate in a highly controlled, "costs justify everything" environment. The President, Cory C. Dunn, has been happy to stay with the old ways even in the IS department. Your users have been content even though you are sensing a growing need to move toward some of the applications they see in competitor's operations. You wonder how much longer the move toward end-user computing can be put off. The trend toward decentralization is clear, and you feel strongly that the company must move in that direction. To do so, however, will require a complete education of the user community, especially in the area of user-defined and developed systems and system integration. At the corporate level there is no linkage between business planning and IS planning. Merlin is definitely in the Support Category of McFarlan's Strategic Grid.

With the steady rise in business, the system that you installed 15 years ago needs to be replaced. You have a severe capacity problem. The system is fully configured, and the manufacturer no longer maintains the operating system. Finally, it has become extremely difficult to find reputable firms to maintain your hardware. Cory has given you authorization and budget to replace the system. You know that she expects the new system to be least disruptive to current process and procedure as possible.

It would be very easy simply to replace the mainframe and continue with business as usual. However, you wonder if this might be an opportunity to introduce end-user computing.

1. What are the issues?

2. Should you take the lead and move toward end-user computing?

SITUATION 15-2
MERLIN PHARMACEUTICS (B)

The introduction of end-user computing at Merlin has met with mixed success. The introduction of an up-to-date word-processing facility was quick and easy. The administrative assistants, department secretaries, and clerical staff took to it quickly. They were thrilled to get rid of the archaic system they had been using for so long. You were also successful in introducing a fully integrated database and accompanying 4GL report generator. It was fairly simple to convert a number of the old systems to menu items that the user could run at will. This off-loaded a large number of applications from the new host to processors at the nodes of the network that you installed to replace the single processor mainframe.

The users have responded well and are now beginning to request the development of new systems. Your intention is to eventually move to an IS environment in which the users can develop their own systems. As an intermediate strategy, you have introduced the notion of the end-user as project manager. Sue Pressant, your senior systems analyst, has been assigned to a project to develop an order entry system. The project manager is Andy Histomeen, one of Merlin's veteran regional sales managers. Andy was chosen because of his interest in learning more about IS and because he seemed to be the most knowledgeable and respected of the eight regional sales managers. Sue and Andy have worked on projects together and seemed to get along quite well. There were better alternatives than the one you chose, but you saw a good opportunity to further your plan. The application did not seem that difficult, and both Andy and Sue were capable.

Sue phoned you earlier about a problem having to do with the order entry system and has just taken her seat at the small conference table in your office. As you join her at the table, you cannot help but notice a sense of frustration in the troubled look on her face. She begins at once, ignoring the usual friendly small talk.

"I've tried to take care of my own problems in dealing with Andy on the order entry system, but I'm just not getting anywhere. I feel that the project is falling behind schedule and that I'm wasting a lot of time. You know that I have 3 other major projects with critical deadlines. I need your help on this one before all 4 projects come down like a house of cards."

You know that Sue has always been able to handle her own projects and problems quite effectively. For her to be in your office asking for help means that the situation is desperate. When you first scheduled the order entry system with Sue she sketched out a Cobol solution that looked like the best approach. When you informed her of your choice of Andy rather than her as project manager and that you wanted the system done in the 4GL, not Cobol, Sue was less than enthusiastic. You had no choice but to take her into your confidence and share your long-range plan for end-user developed systems. She agreed to help, but you know she was not convinced that it was a good idea.

Her complaint was really very simple. Andy had great difficulty making decisions on the functional capabilities of the order entry system. When he made a decision he often changed his mind a few days later.

1. What are you going to do to resolve Sue's complaint, retain Andy as project manager, and keep the project moving along?

2. In retrospect, did you make the correct decision in appointing Andy project manager? What other decision might you have made?

3. Are end-user developed systems a reasonable goal for Merlin Pharmaceutics? If not, why not? If yes, outline a strategy that you would follow to accomplish your goal.

sixteen

☐

End-User
Applications
Development

SITUATION 16-1
BORUM-STRATE, INC. (REVISITED)

Mack N. Tawsch is the Director of Marketing at Borum-Strate, a manufacturer of commercial drill presses. Several months ago he purchased a personal computer for use at home. You were overjoyed when he told you, because you have tried unsuccessfully to get him to use the company facilities ever since he joined Borum-Strate 2 years ago. Recently you noticed that Mack's presentations have taken on a more sophisticated appearance with charts and graphs displaying high level performance data. You are inquisitive, so you asked Mack where he got the material.

"I do it on my personal computer at home," he proudly replied. "In fact, I want to install these applications in my office so that my managers can start using them too."

Needless to say, you are ecstatic. But your enthusiasm soon

wanes as you learn that Mack is using equipment and software that is not compatible with the standards in place at Borum-Strate. You remember how long and hard you had to fight to get the senior management team to reach agreement on the standards and how strict you have been in their enforcement. Getting Mack to use the computer would be a major accomplishment and will certainly benefit you later on, so you are considering taking an exception and supporting his nonstandard application. On the other hand, to take an exception would most likely bring a flood of other requests to support nonstandard applications from those who resisted the standards in the first place, so you are also strongly pulled toward enforcing the standards and risking the loss of Mack as a new and influential user. As a compromise position you have even thought about offering to convert Mack's application to the corporate standard and training him and his staff in its use. The cost and time of this alternative is significant.

1. Evaluate each alternative.

2. How will you resolve this issue?

SITUATION 16-2
BURR & BRITTLE TOOL & DIE COMPANY

You are Mike Rometer, the IS manager at Burr & Brittle. The Production Planning Department is headed by Justin Tyme, a very aggressive, computer-experienced industrial engineer. Justin has always been very effective in using the computer and in getting others to use the computer in their manufacturing-related activities. His involvement with your user community has been so successful that he has recently formed, with your blessing, a manufacturing systems user group. They have been meeting once a month and until very recently have been totally supportive of the policies and procedures that you have established for your information center. More recently your consultants have reported that Justin's group has been evaluating and acquiring hardware and software not supported by the information center and that they are beginning to develop applications using it. The manufacturing systems are so critical to the competitive position of your company that you are not comfortable with the risks that the company is being exposed to. As a

protective measure you asked Sally Forth, your most senior consultant, to attend the meetings of this user group and keep them under
control. Justin was quick to respond that the group did not need nor
does it want any help or interference from the information center.
The issue here is one of guiding end-user computing activity without
appearing heavy-handed.

1. How would you proceed?

SITUATION 16-3
SHADY ACRES LAND DEVELOPMENT CORP.

Sy Yonara spent several years in the division controller's office as
a financial systems analyst. He was the first in the office to get a
microcomputer and quickly became the local expert. His manager,

Stan D'Offisch, was always amazed at how Sy could solve rather complex forecasting problems with little or no difficulty. No one really understood exactly what Sy did, but his models always seemed to be accurate and correct, so no one really questioned his methods. His reputation grew, and eventually the corporate controller found out about Sy's models and began using them for his forecasting needs. As fate would have it, Sy moved on (He is rumored to have joined an expedition that is now somewhere in the Australian Outback.) and one of his models needs modification. (Sy never took the time to document the models and no one ever asked him to.) The corporate controller was due to make a major presentation in 2 weeks and needed the modifications to complete the required analysis. He, of course, went to the division controller's office and asked Stan for help. Stan, of course, came to your office (you are the IS manager) and asked for help.

Here are the alternatives that you have.

1. You can meet the deadline by modifying the program, but at the risk of producing erroneous forecasts.
2. You can rewrite the programs with the assistance of the controller's office staff using supported packages, but you will probably miss the deadline.
3. You can throw the problem back at Stan. It is his system, let him work it out.

1. What would you do?

2. Who has ownership of this system?

3. What would you tell the President about this issue as it relates to a corporate strategy for deciding when end user computing is appropriate?

seventeen

Organizing Information Systems to Support End-User Computing

SITUATION 17-1
CUT-N-PASTE WALLPAPER COMPANY

You are Pat Turnmatcher who started the information center at Cut-n-Paste 5 years ago and continue to serve as its manager. The department is viewed as a complete success at all levels of management, and you are held in very high esteem by the management team. Despite all your successes, you have never been able to get Hugh G. Racer, the Director of Marketing, or anyone in his office to use the information center. Hugh is one of the founding partners of the company and has been successful with the "old ways."

A significant loss of market share due to an aggressive campaign by your major competitor has resulted in the management team insisting on a new direct mail program that will require the development of a rather sophisticated computer-based market segmentation system. The systems and programming manager has referred

Hugh to you, having concluded that the system should be developed by marketing on a LAN with access to both corporate data and public domain data-bases. Hugh has approached you requesting help to develop the system. You have always held to a very strict policy that the information center will help the user learn whatever is needed so that they can develop the system for themselves. You have held to this policy (even in the face of strong opposition from some of the other managers) ever since the information center became operational. Should you stay with this policy and risk further alienation of the marketing department or should you take on the project knowing that Hugh has little interest in learning how to develop the system and will merely be using the information center to get the results asked for. You have every reason to believe that if you give in there will be a flood of requests coming from others who would rather have the information center do it for them.

1. What alternatives do you have?

2. Which will you choose and why?

SITUATION 17-2
IVORY TOWER UNIVERSITY

Ivory Tower University has, in recent years, become very aggressive in its adoption of computer technology across its academic and administrative divisions. On the academic side it uses both mainframe and microcomputing extensively. In the microcomputer area especially, it utilizes an extensive network of minicomputers along with micros in all faculty offices and in its extensive lab facilities. Its students are all required to own or lease their own portable microcomputer, which is provided through the campus computer store. Faculty micros are all connected to the mainframe system to allow for up-loading/down-loading of data.

The administrative division is not as fortunate or sophisticated in its use of the technology. Although its mainframe system is serving the needs of campus administrators, its use of micros has not moved much beyond the word-processing stage. In an effort to expand Ivory Tower's use of the micros, the information services division has just recently networked the micros with the mainframe administrative system so that an environment of up-loading/down-loading is now available to administrators.

The problem facing you, Hal C. N. Daize, the VP of Information Services, is how to provide the necessary micro support to the administrative division when all of the micro expertise is currently in the academic division. The best solution is to hire additional staff, but unfortunately there is a freeze on all new hires and it is not expected to be lifted for at least another year. Mr. Arch N. Emmy, the VP of Administrative Affairs, is not willing to wait that long for a solution. He has been very successful in acquiring the budget to purchase the necessary hardware and software. In fact, he is expecting delivery of it in a matter of weeks. He is a very influential and aggressive person who is known to wield his power and influence whenever he wants to get his way. You know the danger of alienating such a powerful VP. Dr. Val E. Forge, a noted American historian and VP of Academic Affairs, is an easy going yet effective academic officer. She has the support of her deans, department heads, and faculty. Her contributions to Ivory Tower are well known throughout the university community. You have always been satisfied with your past dealings with her. She listens to all the facts and, as a result, has always made informed decisions. He has always felt that she had a good institutional perspective rather than having parochial interests. She has the ear of President Boris Scilley. The current organizational structure is rather simple. There is only one IS department. It has three divisions, each headed by a director reporting to the VP IS: Academic Computing Services, Administrative Systems Support, and Computer Network Services.

1. Identify two alternatives for organizing and implementing the micro support function at Ivory Tower? Compare and contrast them.

2. Which alternative is best and why?

SITUATION 17-3
OTTO ENTRUCK PARTS SUPPLY COMPANY

You are Val Voline, the owner and President of Otto Entruck Parts Supply. You purchased the company 5 years ago from its founder Otto Entruck.

Otto built a fairly successful business by following basically a laissez-faire management style. His philosophy was to hire qualified managers, pay them well, clearly define his expectations for them, and give them plenty of rope. As a result, his managers grew fairly autonomous and coincidentally became very dependent on the computer. Under the encouragement, and with the help of a manager who has long since left the company, each developed his or her own application systems with little thought of ever having to integrate them. Indeed, they were so far ahead of the competition in their use of the computer that they saw no need to vary their approach and basically left one another alone when it came to computer systems development.

You, on the other hand, are used to a very different style of management. When it came to computers, you insisted on a well-developed and thought-out systems development plan. You know the value of systems integration and wanted to move in that direction with your company. Although there was no immediate need (the company was secure for the time being), you know that in the long run, they would have to integrate their systems in order to sustain the competitive advantage they now enjoyed.

1. Should you wait until the need arises for system integration, or should you pay the price now and forge ahead? What are the trade-offs?

2. What would you say to the management team if you were to move ahead now? How might you plan such a conversion?

eighteen

Information Systems as a User Support Entity: Issues and Opportunities

SITUATION 18-1
HIPE, HIPE, AND MOREHIPE AGENCY

You are Sharon Sharalike, the information center manager in the advertising firm of Hipe, Hipe, and Morehipe. You have had an information center in place for several years, and it is very effective in supporting the many managers, professionals, and clerical staff that need information access. It is a program consisting of personal computer support including file up-loading and down-loading to the minicomputer mainframe, a spreadsheet package, a project planning and tracking package, a word-processing package, a presentation graphics package, and a central electronic mail system. You have two people who work full-time in the Information Center; one is a good trainer and communicator, the other is more technically oriented. However, both are good and broadly effective. All equipment is located in the building.

No executive currently is an information center user, though at your last IS planning session with them they independently agreed that all five of them, including the president, should become more computer literate and that the "computer" could tell them some things they might need to know to manage the business better. You believe their support and commitment to be genuine. On the other hand, you know that they do not understand anything about what they will be getting into. Their staffs have always prepared any information they might need. Furthermore, their time will be very limited (they frequently travel or are otherwise out of the building), and their attention span for detail is short. You are right to be very cautious about how to proceed with this program.

1. Do you use the same training and education program for executives as the one that successfully trained other users?

2. Who should provide the training?

3. How do you approach the training; do you begin with product orientation, do you search for the right application, or do you start with conceptual or literacy training?

4. Where and when do you hold your training?

5. What kind of follow-up support do you provide?

6. Do you use the tools you have or do you get extra features (portability, for example)?

7. Do you customize some applications for their specific use?

8. What might some effective applications be?

9. Do you think executive use of the information center will be effective? If not, do you discourage them from using it?

SITUATION 18-2
SNACKS FIFTH AVENUE

You are T. N. Kauphy, the IS manager at Snack's Fifth Avenue. Patty Foors, the manager of your information center, has reported to you that she has recently noticed a dramatic increase in questions related to desktop publishing. Just this morning, Chet R. Cheez, the European Goat Cheese Product Manager, came to Patty's office with a request to install a new graphics package on their desktop system.

Patty was not able to help because her staff was not at all familiar with the operating system on Chet's machine. Except for this problem, the questions have dealt more with the kinds of hardware and software available for different types of applications. At first you were not too concerned, but as you thought about it you recalled how word processing started in your company and how, as IS manager, you eventually solved that problem by standardizing on two packages and one operating system. Your users were upset at first but eventually their grousing and grumbling subsided as they saw that there were no alternatives but to conform. If the signals that Patty has noticed portend of another user uprising regarding an application area, you know that the problem of standardizing desktop publishing will not be solved as easily. Your users are now very sophisticated and will make it a point to defend their choice of software and hardware. You could be in for a real battle.

Snacks Fifth Avenue is a leading mail-order business for the true gourmet. It caters to a very exclusive clientele in the U.S. The items carried in its catalogs are imported from all over the world and in some cases are very expensive and available in limited quantities. To serve its particular clients, Snacks has devised a very sophisticated catalog production system. The actual contents of a catalog are determined based on the buying habits of the clients. That is, Snacks produces a variety of custom-designed catalogs for various market segments defined by the research department. The organization of Snacks Fifth Avenue is very decentralized and is structured around both product groups and client groups. Each group has its own sales and marketing staff as well as purchasing and shipping function. Although the structure may seem somewhat cumbersome, the high level of service demanded by your clients requires it. At the present time your IS function is centralized and all product and client groups pay for any IS services they require. The information center is part of the IS department and offers the traditional training and liaison support.

Rather than be surprised as you were with the word-processing issue, you decided to do some investigating on your own. What you found did surprise you, however. Of the nine product and client groups, four already owned their own desktop publishing systems. How they managed that without your knowledge is another problem you will have to tackle, too! Among those four systems, there were four different vendors' hardware systems and three different software packages. Of the five groups that did not have desktop capabilities, one was borrowing time on another's system to see if they like the technology, two were beginning to investigate purchasing their own systems, and the other two had not shown any interest to date.

1. Should you be concerned about standardization of desktop publishing or should you leave the users alone to fend for themselves? Why?

2. What are the issues that will influence your decision to standardize or not?

3. Assuming you would standardize, what would be included in the policy statement, how would you implement it, and how would you enforce it?

4. Is centralization of desktop publishing a good idea for Snacks Fifth Avenue? Why?

5. How would you standardize desktop publishing if it were to remain decentralized?

PART V

THE FUTURE AND INFORMATION SYSTEMS MANAGEMENT

nineteen

☐

Quality of Work

SITUATION 19-1
SILVER SPOON GOURMET HOME SERVICE

You are Dee Praved, the IS manager for the Silver Spoon Gourmet Home Service. Your company is the largest provider of bicycle food delivery and in-home catering in a large metropolitan area. The heart of your operation is a central bank of phone operators who deal with customers. You have one operator assigned to handle each of the cities many exchanges, with all incoming calls with that exchange prefix routed to the appropriate person and all outgoing calls into that exchange placed by that same person. This way, one person is completely responsible for a specific geographic area in the city.

Operator duties are to take calls placing grocery orders, determine which of the many local merchants should be used, depending of the products required, and then, depending on the designated routing, to call one of the many on-call cyclists not already on a delivery to fill the customer demand as quickly as possible. Silver Spoon's efficiency has made a one-hour delivery fairly standard. This has led to such an increase in volume that it is not unusual to see the streets of the city full of Silver Spoon delivery cyclists about dinner time noticeable in their aluminum colored "Fodder de Leader" windbreakers. Loyal clientele have grown to the point that about one half the time operators are placing scheduled calls to customers asking for their grocery order for the next meal. The computer system schedules these calls, remembers eating habits, and is capable of keeping a pantry inventory by customer. The system is also used to keep track of merchants and their various offerings, prices, hours, and so forth and deliverers by location and status. Silver Spoon executives have become so cocky because of their success that a stated corporate goal is to make grocery shopping obsolete in the city.

The one obstacle to this goal is the availability of operators to handle the calls, especially during the odd hours of your 24-hour operation. Turnover is high from your central downtown facility, and this hurts your ability to build important customer rapport. A task team that you were appointed to head by the President, Pete Zaria, is dealing with one possible solution to this problem—"homework." The Vice President of Human Resources, Bo Napatete, who is on your committee, is a strong proponent of hiring people to work in their home. He knows from you that getting calls routed to phones set up in the operators' homes and installing terminals to tie in to the central computer can easily be done. Bo has trouble hiring people to come to your downtown office even when you pay a premium. He claims he will easily be able to hire many of the right kinds of people under a "homework" scenario with enough good potential employees left over to have backups, hire special shifts for peaks, and cover for vacations.

Another member of your team, Sal Manella, the Vice President of Sales, disagrees. Sal is in charge of the operators and he does not feel that they can work in isolation. They always have complicated questions for the supervisors and need some problem-handling method close at hand. Because they work in a group, when one is sick or away from the phone, the others can cover for him or her. He does not know how he will supervise them if they are so disbursed. Lastly, Sal feels that working groups provide social and job reinforcement.

You could have predicted that the member of your team from finance, Patti Forrs, would see this as a cost/benefit analysis problem. She sees the costs as being delivery of technology to the homes, with savings coming from reduced turnover, the associated training, and a reduction in your wage spiral. She is not sure whether supervisor costs will go up or down. She dismisses customer service as nonquantifiable, but is willing to estimate it or do whatever you want to take it into account in performing a financial analysis.

You are not sure what to do next. You know that the technology is not the problem, defining the workplace of the future is. You can support just about any approach, but wonder if you shouldn't be proactively pushing for a solution you believe to be correct. Now you know that Pete put you in charge to negotiate an agreement out of differing opinions.

1. As chairman, do you state your opinion and lobby for it or try to remain a neutral party?

2. Have all the key issues surrounding working away from an office been brought up? What are some others?

3. How can technology further assist in making remote-site work productive?

4. Which course of action do you recommend and why?

SITUATION 19-2
FLY-BY-NIGHT OVERNIGHT DELIVERY SERVICE

You are Alfredo D. Dark, the IS manager for the Fly-By-Night Overnight Delivery Service, a large corporation that sells guaranteed overnight delivery services for everything from letters to bulldozers. Your company has spent extensively on IS technology during the last 4 years; from sophisticated real-time billing systems and networks supporting nationwide package location systems to automated package movement equipment and parcel-handling robotics. Your department is responsible for successfully designing and installing innovative systems. You are certainly more technically sophisticated than your many rivals. Still, the industry is a very competitive one and Fly-By-Night is not doing well. For some mysterious reason, customers choose other carriers, citing a lack of confidence in Fly-By-Night just at the mention of your name. Market share is dropping despite a strong strategic IS support for your service efforts.

You have just met with your boss, the Chairman of the Board and Chief Executive Officer, Woody Haight-Toulouse to review corporate strategies for increasing revenues. Woody stunned you with an idea that you had not been considering. "We have built a strong IS resource to improve the value of our delivery services," he said, "and it is not working. Maybe we are trying to sell the wrong service. Shouldn't we be marketing the IS resource itself?" He went on to outline his idea to spin the IS department off as a separate company and charge you with the marketing of the IS services in which we have built such skills. You would determine exactly what "products" would be marketed and how it would be marketed. Project management, system integration, consulting, software, time-sharing services, training, and facilities management are just some of the possibilities Woody suggests.

You do not know how to react. You are flattered that Woody trusts you to generate profits directly. Moreover, it certainly meets your personal goal of ensuring that the IS department contributes to the strategic success of Fly-By-Night. It would be a real challenge and could perhaps excite your staff by letting them see some profitable results from their talented efforts.

Another part of you feels quite differently about this strategy. You know that your department is good at what it does now. But running a business requires very different skills. Just because your staff is good at supporting users does not mean that they would be good at selling. There are other things at which you may not be good enough: pricing, new product selection, market analysis, performance-oriented reward structures, legal liability controls, and many others. You are not even 100% sure that your staff will enjoy the pressure of revenue goals, travel, customer management, and abandonment of existing Fly-By-Night users, which might be necessary. These worries contribute to your biggest fear; that you will not be able to make this venture profitable by the end of the first year when Woody expects and needs profits. If necessary, you know that you could convince Woody to abandon the idea. Right now you do not know whether it is a dangerous or a brilliant plan.

1. What are the differences in running an IS department and running an IS business?

2. Might you have something salable, or do customers want something more than just good IS skills?

3. How important are some of the skills you feel you are missing? Are there equivalent IS skills that would be reasonable substitutes?

4. What would you choose to do and why?

5. Should you decide to proceed, which services that you could offer would present the least amount of risk? Which might offer the most risk?

SITUATION 19-3
COLE CACHE COMPUTER MEMORY, INC.

When things get frustrating, it is always possible to take comfort in the fact that you work for such a successful, leading-edge technology company as Cole Cache Computer Memory. Your company was the first to apply Josephson junction technology to add-on memory, thereby allowing data to be preserved in a state of suspended animation in perpetuity. Your concept of "hibernating on-line data" has taken the libraries and archive services by storm. Your patents give you good protection for the key products for the time being. Cole Cache is growing and becoming more profitable every year.

This is partly due to the president, Gil D. Lily, who is as cautious a person as you could imagine. Gil is always trying to eliminate risk and worrying about future problems. Many have accused him of nagging Cole Cache employees into being successful. He has just laid the latest such problem on your doorstep.

You are Justin Case, the IS manager for Cole Cache. You run a highly efficient operation with many new applications of advanced technology; expert systems in marketing, end-user systems in accounting, computer-integrated manufacturing, and so forth. However, Gil has just told you that he is not satisfied with your recent IS plan. "It is just not imaginative enough," he claimed. He feels that Cole Cache should be identifying real leading-edge ideas to help in product development, office productivity, IS productivity, customer relations, industry relations, and so forth. Gil has a wild and diverse company strategic plan, and he wants more immediate IS support for it.

Your problem is that you worked hard through a laborious planning process to get as many new ideas as you did into the current IS plan. In the past, users generally have initiated new system ideas through the planning process and, despite Gil's recent urging them on, they were just out of ideas during the last IS planning cycle.

Your staff has been no help in this regard. Your manager in charge of planning and new technology (a staff position reporting to you) is Warren Pease, a brilliant guy but someone who is not too good at imagining the sophisticated technology he understands in practical uses. Your systems and programming manager, Hugh N. Kry, is still trying to get past strategic systems under control and his staff's skill level up to speed, so he has not been feeding ideas to users like he used to do. Likewise, you have been spending the last year, at the direction of the Chief Financial Officer (and your boss) Penny Pincher, overseeing the tightening up of controls on these new systems. Therefore, your mind has not been thinking too expansively either.

Now Gil, using his strong dotted line to you, has asked (Gil is a reasonable boss) you to rebuild the IS plan in order to make it more "creative." There is a very creative company plan to draw on but that was available before to a crew of user executives and IS managers who have just published a document that Gil does not like. You are not sure what you will do this time that will make a difference.

1. Is Gil asking the company to be more imaginative than is appropriate to its current condition?

2. Do you feel that the structure of an IS planning process permits the kind of creativity that Gil is looking for? Would you suggest another process to Gil?

3. Does the company climate seem right for inventive thinking? If not, can you help change it, or is this exclusively Gil's job?

4. What action would you take?

5. How would you involve Penny? How would you involve Warren? How about Hugh?

twenty

Quality of Life

SITUATION 20-1

KYZ AND MAYCUP MARRIAGE COUNSELORS, INC.

You are Ima Q. Pidd, the IS manager for the Kyz and Maycup Marriage Counselors, Inc., a national chain of offices specializing in assistance to troubled marriages. Each office is helped by the national office (where you work) in many ways. First, for new clients, you enter all pertinent data on your computer for analysis and accounting functions. Second, Kyz and Maycup has a national hotline service that generates leads for the local offices. Lastly, there is a major data-base search capability for use in problem-client situations. Using a recently installed fourth-generation query language that users find very popular, it permits authorized local office personnel to request reports from the central data-base. These systems allows K and M to stand behind their advertised guarantee "We guarantee to make you happy with your spouse or get you a new one." Unhappy clients are helped by a subsidiary of K and M, the Happy Union Dating Bureau (Motto: Don't play with "matches."), which accesses the central data-base for potential available partners for the client. K and M have been successful making these related businesses work profitably. It rests on the accuracy and proprietary nature of the data.

Of course, your role is critical, and you are looked on as a key executive and a competent custodian of a somewhat mysterious discipline. Therefore, you are not too surprised when you are called into Al E. Mony's office. Al, the president and your boss, is extremely upset. He has just been informed by Mary N. Haste, the Vice President of Marketing, that "a computer crime has been committed." Mary reported that field offices have clear evidence that competitors have been using customer information that could only have come from your data-base. Al believes that it is obviously a technical leak and wants you to find it and fix it. Furthermore, he is worried that competitors or saboteurs may have corrupted current customer data. He wants you to make sure that all data is safe.

You are not sure how to proceed. You know that even though you have many controls and protections, they are not perfect and data could be electronically removed or copied during transmission to or from branch offices. Your guess is that this would require so much sophistication as to be unlikely. You think it is more likely that one of the many printed office reports fell into the wrong hands or that K and M employees with data-base access may be passing on confidential information. As for someone secretly destroying your data you feel that is a different kind of crime and not only inconsistent with the discovered theft but even more unlikely.

Al has been convinced by Mary that this occurrence is extremely serious; survival threatening; and it may well be. So you are unsure of how to approach Al. If you explain some of the other possibilities, you may be seen as shifting blame. If you just look for leaks in the computer system, you may never be able to prove they are not there. Then only technology will be suspect, and the real cause may go forever undiscovered.

1. How would you go about verifying the integrity of your system? How would you check the accuracy of your data?

2. What kind of controls and security features would be appropriate for such a company?

3. How would you proceed? What would you do first? What would you tell Al? How fast would you or could you react?

4. What should your responsibility be in the event of a discovered breach of security? What power should you have in the investigation?

5. Are you remiss in not having prepared for such an eventuality?

SITUATION 20-2

SPORTING CHANCE RAQUET CLUB

You are Jim Nastick, the IS manager for the Sporting Chance Racquet Club, a large chain of fitness centers and sporting-goods stores. The company is in a very competitive industry but is betting its future on its ability to grow and is investing for it. You have only been with the company for 6 months but already you are working closely with your boss, Bo Linball, the President, on many of his ideas for automation. When you arrived you found extensive use of

personal computers but not much beyond traditional batch accounting operations and on-line status query to support the office
activities. So you were excited to accept your current job working for
a person who has plans for automation. That is until this morning.

You and Bo had a private meeting where he shared his intentions
for the next major IS department effort. He essentially wants to
automate the customer service department and eliminate 90% of the
jobs. Now many people answer queries from franchisees on account
status and order status. Bo wants to install computer driven voice
response systems that will answer the standard queries automati-
cally. He makes a special point of asking you for complete confiden-
tiality because not only would the news be badly received by the
department and by Jacques Strop, the Vice President in charge, but
Bo knows that your spouse works in this department and is very
attached to the job.

Bo is disappointed when you do not respond to his plans with more
cooperation. In fact, you declare that you are opposed to the idea. You
point out that there are more important, more beneficial projects to
do, especially a sorely needed franchise customer-management
system that supposedly would help them increase membership. You
point out that the numbers Bo showed you indicate that automation
is at best a break-even proposition for current business volumes.
You claim that such a project would create a terrible precedent for
automation at Sporting Chance and hurt your prospects for future
projects. Finally, you state that you do not believe this is the right way
to use technology, just eliminating jobs when other, more popular,
opportunities are available. Bo is obviously hurt by you impugning
his ethical values and politely reminds you that he has a tough job
trying to create long-term company stability and that you must
support his judgment. He claims that you might be ignoring what is
good for the business in favor of solutions that are personally or
politically popular. Bo wants you to think about it, but your concerns
have not changed his mind.

After the meeting you reflect on the situation you find yourself in.
You know that Bo is not insensitive to ethical issues. After all, he
supported you on your arrival when you stopped the common
company practice of illegally copying PC software, which everyone,
including Jacques, the popular Vice President of Franchise Relations, was openly doing. However, the fact that it was so obliviously
allowed to happen before your arrival coupled with this latest
indication of direction, convinces you that Bo and you have different
values when it comes to the proper uses of technology. On the one

hand you want to be practical and business oriented. At the same time, you do not want to compromise important values. Right now it is not clear to you whether Bo's project is just unpleasant to you or down-right inconsistent with your professional values.

1. How do you personally feel about conforming to Bo's request?

2. What action would you take?

3. Realistically, does the personal issue of your spouse influence your opinion?

SITUATION 20-3
TWILIGHT TIME

You are Drew P. Droors and are retiring after a long and successful career as the IS manager for Twilight Time Industries, an international marketer and manufacturer of sleep aids. You started with them as a programmer almost 30 years ago and worked your way up to the top IS job, which you have held for the last 12 years. During that time you have modernized Twilight Time's use of automation and made their deployment of technology a critical factor in their business success by supporting the design of new products and through improved customer service. You have streamlined their production process, made the office operation more efficient, and pioneered their sophisticated executive decision-making system. At your retirement dinner, all the company executives recounted by way of testimonial how you have made the use of technology an integral part of the Twilight Time strategy and their planning process. In the past year, you have even been lionized by the professional trade journals as a model of successful IS management.

You are proud that your family is in full attendance at the formal affair. You are particularly pleased that your favorite nephew, Theopholus Nameoval, is seated beside you to talk with during dinner. He has just graduated from high school with honors and has the personality, the energy, and the intelligence to indicate that he will be a great success at whatever he undertakes. So you are especially glad when he tells you that he would like to follow in your shoes and someday become an IS manager. Therefore, he asks if you think "IS is right for" him. If so, he would like your advice on how to successfully pursue this ambition. You think for a long time before answering because you know that things have changed a great deal since you entered the field. It contains different rewards and problems. Your path may no longer be appropriate. You realize that if you can impart the correct guidance that you just might have made your most important contribution to the field of IS management. You also want what is best for Theopholous.

1. Can you unequivocally endorse an IS career for Theopholous? Aren't there more rewarding career paths to consider?

2. Why would you or why wouldn't you recommend an IS career to someone with Theopholous's potential?

3. What educational experience would you suggest?

4. What job preparation would you recommend?

5. What values should he hold as important? What behaviors?

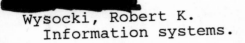